# THE HEART ARSONIST

# The Heart Arsonist

lessons from a heart set on fire

Joseph Raby

Unless otherwise indicated, all Scripture quotations are taken from the Holy Bible, New Living Translation, copyright © 1996, 2004, 2007, 2013, 2015 by Tyndale House Foundation. Used by permission of Tyndale House Publishers, Inc., Carol Stream, Illinois 60188. All rights reserved.

Scripture quotations marked MSG are taken from THE MESSAGE, copyright © 1993, 1994, 1995, 1996, 2000, 2001, 2002 by Eugene H. Peterson. Used by permission of NavPress. All rights reserved. Represented by Tyndale House Publishers, Inc.

Cover Design by Joseph Raby and Jonathan Raby

*To Michelle – You are my GOOD THING and the spark that started the fire inside of me.*

# Contents

# DISCLAIMER

During the course of reading this book you may experience growing pains, moments of question, a shift in your mindset, or even a desire to begin to make a change.

These are all good things and I'm excited for you if these occur. I can tell you that writing this book has produced all of these in me as well.

While you read, please share those parts that impact you. Post your favorite chapters, quotes, etc. on social media. Be sure to tag me and use #HeartArsonist, #BurnBright, or #ThrowSparks to help spread the word. Or send me an email with your feedback. I'd love to hear from you!

Facebook – Joseph.raby.50
Instagram – @joeyraby
Email – josephtraby@gmail.com

# The Spark

I always said I wanted to write a book. I first got bitten by the writing bug in junior high, when my best friend Dave and I wrote a short story called "The House on Haunted Hill". I think we sold 2 or 3 (pity) copies to our friends who most likely threw them into the garbage shortly after. Most of our grade school "romances" had a longer shelf life than our literary works did.

It wasn't until high school I realized how deep the fangs of the written word had sunk in. I wrote scribbles about all the things a teenage writer does – love, loss, faith, angst, and life. I had a limited frame of reference for what it meant to be a writer. It didn't matter though. I kept cutting the paper with my pen and the words continued to bleed though.

Scribbles turned to journal entries.

Journal entries turned into poems.

Poems turned into songs.

Songs turned into essays.

Essays turned into chapters.

The following chapters are some of the lessons I have learned and some I'm still in the process of learning. I am honored that you would read along and join me on the journey.

The writing of this book has been several years in the making. It's been a labor of love and hate. My index finger has hovered over the delete key many times, ready to drop the hammer and put an end to my train of thought before it even leaves the station. Even as I'm typing this, my hands are trying to recoil from the keyboard. It's as though they don't want me to admit that I'm not perfect. But I feel like with every keystroke, there's a hammer driving the chisel deeper into the stone that surrounds my heart like a fortress. Each blow splintering the exterior to expose what is buried deep within. So, I press on.

God has an amazing track record for using those who aren't the most qualified. He loves the underdog. If that's my assignment, then I'll accept it with open hands.

Not too long ago, I shared the idea for this book with my friend Joshua Medcalf, who has been quite successful in his own writing and career. His advice was simple and blunt. Even though he thought it was a great idea, he said I didn't need to write a book. What I needed to do was to get over my fear (in more colorful language) and "just hit publish". Be faithful to the process.

Besides, he told me "it takes an average of 3 years to get everything together and be ready to publish."

After talking with him (and getting over the fact I wanted to punch him in the face), I contemplated what he said. I let it sink in.

What I realized was these lessons and the words in this book have been a lifetime of learning and preparing. Of failing and coming back stronger; of victories and crashing into the wall of defeat (sometimes at breakneck speed). It wasn't about writing a book. It wasn't about the product. It was about what I learned as I wrote. It was about the process God was taking me though.

So I decided to press in to the process. Even if these words never saw the light of day to plant seeds in someone else's heart who was seeking encouragement, it would hopefully help move me closer to becoming the man God created me to be. And ultimately bring glory to Him.

Maybe Joshua was right. Maybe I don't need to write this book. Maybe these are just the things that God is teaching my heart in order to heal me and move me more towards the person that He created me to be. But I have a sneaking suspicion that if God wants me to learn these lessons, there is someone else who may need to hear the same. You could be reading these words now.

If so, THANK YOU for picking up this book. This book is meant to be a fire starter – a catalyst. It is meant to hopefully nudge you toward opening your heart and mind up to all that God intends for your life. He is the only one who can truly change any of us. So I encourage you to dig in and discover the one true God who created you and loves you beyond what you can comprehend.

It's a never ending process.

As I've dug deeper into what God has been teaching me (not just the writing but the practice) my life has gotten anything but easier. There have been many days where I've felt like a fighter on the losing end of a title bout – struggling to find the ropes and get back on my feet. On more than a few occasions, I was secretly hoping for someone in my corner to throw in the towel. I'm grateful they didn't.

My marriage has been challenged.

My relationship with my kids has been challenged.

The way others view me has been challenged.

The way I view others has been challenged.

The way I view myself has been challenged.

My view of Jesus as my savior however, has never changed. Through the storms and pressures of life however, my view of Him as my Lord of my life has grown by leaps and bounds.

Romans 5:3-5 has a whole new meaning to me as I've traversed this road.

───────

*3 We can rejoice, too, when we run into problems and trials, for we know that they help us develop endurance. 4 And endurance develops strength of character, and character strengthens our confident hope of salvation. 5 And this hope will not lead to disappointment. For we know how dearly God loves us, because he has given us the Holy Spirit to fill our hearts with his love.*

———————

I feel that God is giving me new eyes to see into His heart. This small glimpse has begun to change me in ways that I could never fathom. It's changing my perspective of my Heavenly Father, of others and of myself. It's as if He's taking my heart in between His nail scarred hands and is massaging it back to life, forming it into a new creation as only a potter can.

Even if you don't believe what I believe, I hope you find encouragement in the following pages. I hope you see not only the God who created you and loves you in a new way, but you see yourself through new eyes as well. I pray your thoughts, your heart and how you live be radically transformed into the person you were created to be.

If those things take place, please don't give me credit. Give it to the one who hung the moon and the stars. He wrote the words, I just typed them.

Burn Bright,
Joseph Raby

P.S. The words in this book will sound a lot better and make more sense when enjoyed with a piping hot cup of your favorite Java.

I

# \ ÄR-SƏN\

---

noun

*The crime of intentionally starting a fire in order to damage
or destroy something*

---

# 2

# THE HEART ARSONIST

———————

I remember riding in the car with my parents when I was little and seeing fields burning along the side of the road, wondering what was going on. It made absolutely no sense to me. Why would a farmer burn his field when it produces and provides for their family?

What I learned was these "controlled burns" are extremely effective at recycling nutrients that are tied up in old plant growth. They actually encourage healthy growth by eliminating competition from weeds. A better crop yield results from incinerating the areas that would hinder growth. For all intents and purposes, these farmers were committing a controlled act of arson.

———————

Controlled burns are often used in forestry to eliminate the possibility of hotter fires in the future. By clearing out the underbrush, these controlled burns reduce the chances of more severe wildfires. They protect the large trees and keep more carbon locked up in the forest. They also reduce the amount of carbon dioxide released into the atmosphere.

As I've gotten older, I've realized this is what Jesus wants to do in our hearts. Jesus was the original heart arsonist. His mission was to get straight to the heart of people and burn away anything that was holding them captive. He still wants to and does this today. He doesn't just want our heads. He wants our hearts. He doesn't want the weeds to suffocate the growth of our future and His Kingdom.

I want to be a heart arsonist. And I'm hoping I can recruit you to join me. Before you close this book and throw it in the fire, or close the app on whatever device you're using, please dare to read on. The first 100 copies have been soaked in gasoline (just kidding).

I want to take aim at your heart. I want to strike a match and light a fire burning all the debris that has strangled the life out of you. I want to start a 5-alarm blaze that, once done, will consume all the limitations you or anyone else has spoken into or over your life, and will leave a heart burning with passion, hope and endless possibilities. I want to start a fire so hot it allows you to live the life of purpose you are designed for.

What does it look like to be a heart arsonist?

If you let God set fire to your heart, your dreams, and passions, that blaze can overtake your life and spark others around you to ignite too. Too many times we let other's words, opinions, and negativity squelch these flames before they even flirt with burning the underbrush. Too many times we become comfortable sitting in bondage.

If we examined our lives, we could all find areas of old growth that are hindering us from stepping into the areas of greatness that God has for each of us. We need to let God issue a controlled burn on those areas in order to see the fruit he has planted in us flourish in unbelievable ways. This can change the environment in which we live.

What are those areas in your life?

What areas does God need to set ablaze for you to live a life engulfed in the freedom only found in Him?

Pride?

Control?

Anger?

Lust?

Bitterness?

Addiction?

Fear?

Depression?

The list could go on and on. And each of our lists will be different. Are we ready to let Him burn these things away? I hope so.

It doesn't matter what side of the climate change debate

you sit on. I think we can all agree this world needs to see a change in the climate of our hearts. The only way for this to happen and have sustainable, lasting effects is to allow God to start a controlled burn on each of our lives. When this controlled burn happens, we are free to live the life we are designed for. We can live out our purpose and experience true freedom that only the God of Heaven can give.

Religious people hate the freedom and the power of grace. That's why they heap on rules and regulations. Jesus however, embodies radical grace AND reckless love! In Christ we have true freedom. Even the freedom to make a mess of our own lives if we want (I'm not encouraging this). There have been so many times in my life where I get frustrated with someone when they don't live up to my expectations. A good way to tell what is truly in our hearts is how we react when someone in our life walks in the flesh. Do we rush for a brick to condemn them, or a bandage to help heal them?

If we are in the habit of compartmentalizing the grace we give, those around us will get into the habit of compartmentalizing the love they share with us. Radical grace is the driver of radical love. Jesus didn't withhold grace from us. So why is it so easy for us to withhold grace from those around us? We all desperately need to follow His example. He gives freely and so should we.

I want to know the heart of Jesus. I want you to know the heart of Jesus too. Not the Jesus that we often try to make Him into, so He fits into our lifestyle; but who Jesus really is. I want to know how living a life where our hearts burn just like His can make this world truly heaven on earth.

One thing is for sure, if we ask Jesus to really set us on fire, we need to be ready. A seasoned arsonist knows how to set a fire and get it to spread quickly.

# 3

# FIRE STARTER

———————

This little light of mine
   I'm gonna let it shine
   This little light of mine
   I'm gonna let it shine
   This little light of mine
   I'm gonna let it shine
   Let it shine, let it shine, let it shine

I learned this song as a little kid. I don't honestly remember if it was my parents or a Sunday school teacher who taught it to me first. I guess it probably doesn't matter much either way. We've even taught it to, and sung it with our kids.

It wasn't until recently that I had a realization about this song (at least what the Lord was telling me). As God has been teaching me more about the condition of my own heart and what I feel is His desire for the heart of everyone on this earth, I've been hearing this phrase over and over.

---

*Your little light is OK, but I am an all-consuming fire. I want you to burn so brightly for me that darkness can't even stand in my presence.*

---

Our little light is a great place to start. But as we press in more to the father's heart, learning to look more like and love more like him (the two are not mutually exclusive), our little light should turn into a full-on blaze.

When we are listening to the voice of the Holy Spirit and following where He tells us to go, our "little light" starts to cause others to ignite and burn too. One of the dangerous things about a fire, especially one that is burning uncontrollably, is that it can spread – sometimes very quickly. And when it does, it can be very difficult to contain. I've seen the results of this first hand living in Northern California. You see, when wood is put onto a fire, as it burns and pops, sparks result. As these sparks jump and claim new territory, there is the chance that another fire could start. I want to be a fire that throws sparks.

We may not know it, but we are all throwing sparks every day:

With the words we say.

With the attitudes we carry with us.

With our actions and reactions to the people that we interact with.

This raises the question. What kind of fires are we starting? For me, reflecting on this question is humbling. I know I've started my share of nasty fires. Ones that I wish would have been extinguished before they got the chance to spread.

Our lives are the single greatest tool that God has given us to witness His Gospel to the world we live in.

There are a lot of people that may never step foot in a church to hear the message of Christ. But those same people may go out to dinner with you and your spouse. They might go bowling with you. You might attend the same birthday party with your kids. More ministry is done outside of the walls of the church than inside.

We live in a society where we are becoming more energy conscious – where we all about conserving energy. In our house, we are constantly checking to make sure that we have turned off the lights when we leave a room or when we are leaving the house. My wife is even so good about this she has turned the lights out on people in the bathroom at church on more than one occasion! She thought it was embarrassing. To me, it was hilarious!

When it comes to how we live our lives however, we

can't afford to turn out the light. Jesus came so all men might be saved. We are the vessels that He has chosen to use.

THROW SPARKS!

4

# FROM THE HEAD TO THE HEART

---

I've gotten to work with thousands of individuals as a fitness professional over the last 12 years; young, old, athletes, weekend warriors, chronic pain patients, cancer survivors and even myself (my most difficult client). One thing we all have in common is we need to establish good posture as the foundation for everything we do. It makes us stable and stronger. It reduces chance of injury and even makes us more alert.

The symptoms of poor posture rarely occur immediately. They build up over time. Eventually though, cracks start to form and our body weakens. We begin developing chinks in our armor. Before we know it, those errant moves will come to a head and we end up down for the count.

Our journey to know Jesus more and have a heart that looks and loves more like Him is no different (and many of the same benefits apply).

*Is our purpose, our heart aligned with the heart of Jesus?*

*Are we willing to extend and give love and grace like Jesus to become stronger?*

*Are we willing to work to change the world around us and truly become the hands and feet of Jesus?*

To experience a transforming relationship with Jesus Christ it is *not about head knowledge. It's about heart posture.* The Pharisees knew the Scriptures inside and out and spent their lifetime studying them. When they were face to face with the Son of God though, they couldn't see past their intellect to see the truth. The phrase "can't see the forest for the trees" comes to mind. Jesus called them "whitewashed tombs" and told them they were full of "dead people's bones" (Matthew 23:27).

These guys were smart. They knew the material and were probably the best test takers of their time. That's all fine, well, and good, but how did they fall so short on applying what they had learned? Religion was their job. But Jesus wanted their every day. He didn't care about what was in their heads. He cared about what was in their hearts.

I've been there. Most of what I learned in school, I forgot once I handed in the test sheet. Sad, but true. Some of the most important and life altering principles I've learned in my more than 37 years on this earth were learned in the trenches. Jesus wasn't afraid to play in the dirt, literally (Read John 1:9-6). We shouldn't be either.

What happens when the teachings of Jesus shift from our heads to our hearts? Intellectually, I know Jesus is Lord. He gave up heaven and all His glory to come to earth. He was born, lived, died, and gave death a sucker punch like no other and came back to life. Even though I know this is truth, sometimes it's hard for me and my analytical nature to let it fully soak into my heart. I've found that love and logic don't always see eye-to-eye.

To obey is a condition of the will.

*To LOVE to obey, is a condition of the heart.*

To serve is a condition of the will.

*To LOVE to serve, is a condition of the heart.*

It's a matter of foundation. It's a matter of heart posture. It's a matter of true surrender.

Jesus is inviting us into a relationship not a religion. He doesn't just want our heads. He wants our hearts.

My prayer is that I let this shift take place every day. I invite you to say this simple prayer, with me to start the day.

*Jesus, give me the courage to let you occupy the space in my heart that my head already knows you belong in. I'm all yours. Amen.*

# 5

# EVOLUTION

———

I believe in evolution. I think Jesus believes in evolution. If this seems a bit controversial, I hope you read on. I promise this is going somewhere. The most common definition of evolution (and the one that makes the hair on the back of people's neck stand up), per Google, goes like this:

> *"The process by which different kinds of living organisms are thought to have developed and diversified from earlier forms during the history of the earth."*[1]

———

1. https://www.google.com/webhp?sourceid=chrome-instant&ion=1&espv=2&ie=UTF-8#q=Evolution+definition

I think a more appropriate definition for what we are discussing is as follows (also from Google):

*"The gradual development of something, especially from a simple to a more complex form."*[2]

Please allow me to explain. I believe we are all changing and growing into the people we were created to be. We were created in the image of God. His breath is in our lungs. I believe we all need to be saturated in the process of evolution when it comes to our capacity and ability to love.

I believe God is calling us (with a loud voice), to dive deeper into what it means, looks and feels like to love the way He does. His love is not a simple love. Our understanding and our application of love is. He wants to move us to a more complex understanding and application of love.

He wants us all to GROW.

He wants us all to evolve.

The hardest (for me) and most critical step in this process though, is admitting that we don't understand love. This is not a sign of weakness. When we can acknowledge our areas of continued learning, we open ourselves up for growth. Like in the gym, if we know where we have a weakness (area of growth), we can target that area to get stronger.

2. https://www.google.com/webhp?sourceid=chrome-instant&ion=1&espv=2&ie=UTF-8#q=Evolution+definition

Jesus was and still is the ultimate display of love, no matter the circumstance. He gave up Heaven and came to the Earth to be mocked, beaten, and die for all humanity. Even though he knew some would still reject His love, He gave His life anyway. Stop and think about that. It makes little sense to our minds. But how amazing is that truth!

When I married Michelle, I swore that I would do anything for her. I would be there for her, no matter what, and always put her interests before mine. What I learned though, is that I am selfish. Does the fact I have fallen short on this promise make me a liar? No, it makes me human. These are just a few things I am learning about myself.

If I feel hurt, I have a sometimes shut down.

I sometimes argue just to argue.

I'm opinionated.

I talk too much.

I don't listen enough.

I have a short fuse.

I like things my way.

I don't like to admit when I'm wrong.

These areas of growth in my life have caused more than a couple of rocky patches for us. Sometimes it's harder than I want to admit. We have an amazing marriage because we constantly strive to love each other the way that Christ loves us (and we have an amazing counselor). Still, it isn't always easy to love:

Unconditionally.

Recklessly.

Passionately.

Without fail.

This is how Jesus loves. Even though we may or may not return His love, He still loves us. His love is not something we can escape. Still, we have a choice.

How do we begin to evolve in our love so that it so closely resembles Jesus that you can see no difference between our heart and His? I'm convinced that it starts deep in the recesses of our hearts. It starts in the areas that we have tucked away and guarded with military grade force. It starts with forgiveness. And as we journey together, you'll find out this is only the "tip of the iceberg". I found so much more buried below the surface of the seemingly calm waters of my reflecting pool I didn't know were there.

We are deputized agents of forgiveness but too many times we can't even forgive those in our lives that have wronged us. Sometimes we can't even forgive ourselves.

Jesus' mission is entrenched in forgiveness and love. He's already covered it all. It's not about safety. It's about security for your soul. Jesus' vision pierces beyond our actions straight to the motives of our heart. He sees us at the heart level.

I want to find out more.

More about who I am at the heart level.

More about who God created me to be.

I want to pray a dangerous prayer like King David.

*Investigate my life, O God, find out everything about me; Cross-examine and test me, get a clear picture of what I'm about; See for yourself whether I've done anything wrong — then guide me on the road to eternal life. (Psalms 139:23-24 MSG)*

---

God already knows everything in our hearts, so He is not going to discover any new evidence that we might have tried to bury. Our prayer should be our cry, asking God to show us all the evidence against us. What does our rap sheet look like? Our prayer should be to ask Him to guide us in the way that leads to life in Him – to let Him burn away those areas that are hindering our growth.

It's going to be scary. There are going to be some bumps in the road. It will reveal things about us we didn't know. It will shine a spotlight on things we don't want others to know. It will reveal our imperfections. But it will bring us closer to a heart that beats in rhythm with the author of life.

I want to learn more about the Father's heart and I hope that you do too. If so, let's start with these simple (but not easy) steps.

*We have to submit:* I don't always deal well with authority and it has gotten me in trouble more than once in my life. It's not always a blatant push back or mutiny, but more often my attitude and perception of how I think things should work. It is impossible for love to function where there is no submission. True submission is a sign of love, not of weakness.

*Forget Reciprocity:* If we only love others when we feel loved, we are falling short of the love we are called to reflect as followers of Christ. We need the power of the Holy Spirit. He is our advocate, our helper, our connection to the source of power that will never let us run out of charge. Without Him we will always fall short. But with Him anything is possible (Philippians 4:13).

*Realize that it's not about us:* We all need to realize that how we love is a direct reflection on how others perceive Jesus to be. Are we being a good return on His investment (death and resurrection) in each of us? Are we driving others further from a relationship with the Father? Or are we reflecting the heart of Jesus so brightly that we burn so brightly that our flame sparks a similar fire in the hearts and lives of others.

I don't have all the answers. And I'm OK with it. But I know the one who does. He wants to reveal his heart to us. But we need to ask, listen, and apply.

We need to be ready to EVOLve.

6

# WHAT SPINAL TAP TAUGHT ME ABOUT GOD

———

At one point in my life I had aspirations of being a famous musician. Along with 4 of my best friends, we set out to make this dream a reality. From playing in little bars to less than 20 people to opening for multi-platinum recording artists, we were having a blast. We even beat out some major artists on the top 5 countdown several nights in a row! We thought it was cool (still do).

Then it came to an end.

There was no drama. No one getting screwed out of money or taking someone's girlfriend. No bad blood. We felt it ran its course and we all moved on. I loved my time with these guys—my brothers and I'm so thrilled they are all living amazing lives today. Jeremy, Doug, Kevin and Mark, I love you guys!

Maybe there's a reunion show in the cards. Who knows?

During this time, we also discovered Rob Reiner's iconic rock mockumentary "This Is Spinal Tap"[1].

One of my all-time favorite scenes is when filmmaker Marty DeBergi is discussing the dials on the guitar amps with Nigel Tufnel. The scene goes like this,

———

*Nigel Tufnel: The numbers all go to eleven. Look, right across the board, eleven, eleven, eleven and...*

*Marty DiBergi: Oh, I see. And most amps go up to ten?*

*Nigel Tufnel: Exactly.*

*Marty DiBergi: Does that mean it's louder? Is it any louder?*

*Nigel Tufnel: Well, it's one louder, isn't it? It's not ten. You see, most blokes, you know, will be playing at ten. You're on ten here, all the way up, all the way up, all the way up, you're on ten on your guitar. Where can you go from there? Where?*

*Marty DiBergi: I don't know.*

*Nigel Tufnel: Nowhere. Exactly. What we do is, if we need that extra push over the cliff, you know what we do?*

*Marty DiBergi: Put it up to eleven.*

*Nigel Tufnel: Eleven. Exactly. One louder.*

———

1. This is Spinal Tap, directed by Rob Reiner (Embassy Pictures, 1984)

*Marty DiBergi: Why don't you just make ten louder and make ten be the top number and make that a little louder?*

*Nigel Tufnel: [pause] These go to eleven.*

---

I know what you might be thinking. "What does Spinal Tap have to do with loving more like Jesus?"

Well I'm glad you asked.

So many times in this life we only love to the top of what we think our highest factory preset is (10 in this case). Sometimes I feel like I don't even make it to a 7. If we are telling our spouse we love them, providing for our family, going to church, giving to the poor, clothing the naked, etc., we honestly believe that we are giving all we have to give. Based on the dial on our amp (and in our minds), we are screaming loudly at a 10. There might not even be any feedback.

Jesus though, is calling us to give it "just that extra push over the cliff".

He wants us to love at an 11 (or more). Jesus didn't settle for loving at a 10. Yes, he performed miracles and he forgave the sins of the world. These are things that only the Son of God can do.

But he also got down in the dirt of our humanity. He lived in our struggles and temptations. He wasn't afraid to get his hands dirty and smear mud on the blind man's eyes to restore his sight (John 9:6). And then Jesus just sneaks away (John 9:35–41).

Can you imagine what it must have been like for the blind man that the first person he saw was the Son of the Living God!

Jesus wasn't afraid to kneel on the hard floor at dinner and wash his best friend's feet (John 13:1-17). Jesus' love was so extravagant. He went so far as to stretch his arms out on a cross, beaten beyond all recognition, and give His life for you and for me. He didn't just love the ones that loved Him. *He just loved.*

Talk about loving to 11!

I hope and pray this measure of extravagant love is the mark you and I leave on this world when we leave. I hope there is no question about whether we gave everything we had to those we served – in our homes, churches, jobs, and everywhere we walked.

# 7

# WHERE THERE'S SMOKE THERE'S FIRE

Growing up in a house of 4 boys, you can imagine that there were not very many dull days. I'm sure the stories we have could fill more than a few volumes. We deliberately waited to share many of these stories (I like to refer to them as life experiences) with our parents after we had all gotten older, mainly for the fact they can't punish us anymore! And if they would have known then, they would have stopped us and ruined all our fun!

One of my favorites is a fire-bug-in-training story with my brother Jeremy playing the lead role.

We were living in a little rental house in the country of rural Southern Illinois. Since we were surrounded by fields (corn, wheat, or beans – depending on the year), we got to spend most of our days exploring the great outdoors uninhibited and unrestrained. We didn't have cell phones, or iPads. We were curious and loved to explore and get dirty. I think this played an essential role in our sense of adventure and I hope that my children get to experience that same joy as they are growing up.

One day our mom was heading down to the basement to do a load of laundry (a never-ending task in our household). As she rounded the corner at the bottom of the stairs, she noticed a faint smell of smoke and a pile of burnt matches lying under the stairwell. As you can imagine, she went into full-on Sherlock Holmes mode with my brothers and me. She didn't shine the light on us or try to make us sweat it out in fear in the interrogation room, but for a 10, 6- and 4-year-old it sure felt like it (our baby brother got off the hook easy – he was still in Huggies).

After what seemed like an endless and grueling interrogation (more like 10-15 minutes), Jeremy cracked. He admitted that it was him. Whew! We let out a sigh of relief. The culprit was caught.

When I was talking to him about this story not long ago, I had to ask "Do you remember why you were hiding and lighting the matches in the first place?"

He told me "I don't think there was any deep meaning

behind it. I was just a little boy who learned how to strike a match and thought fire was cool".

Even 25+ years later, a few things stand out about this story. He knew he wasn't supposed to be playing with the matches, so he hid. Second, the flame fascinated him – intense, hot, intriguing. He knew if he didn't blow it out before it got to his 6-year-old fingertips, it would hurt.

My brother came by his fire bug nature honestly. Growing up I remember watching our dad dump gasoline on the burn pile to ignite things quickly. Watching the little trail of gas just outside of the pile creep closer and closer until it exploded into flames was exciting for little guys like us.

This wasn't just something we saw our dad model for lighting a bonfire or trash pile though (Yep, we grew up in the country). He modeled this for us in his walk with Christ too.

There are 3 things I learned from my dad that stand out to me (more on learning from daddy later).

1. *Always live authentically:* Good or bad, people value and respect authenticity. Be you: nothing more nothing less.
2. *Things that can hurt us can be intriguing:* Bright lights and greener grass can be alluring. They aren't always what they seem though. If you want the grass to be greener where you are, add some fertilizer and water it.

3. *If we play with fire, eventually we will get burned:* I think this one speaks for itself.

Did he always get it right? No way! None of us do. But he did the best with what he had and always tried to make sure he was modeling the love of Jesus for his boys. We never questioned where the fire that burned inside of him came from. And for that, I respect the heck out of him.

These principles are not always easy to adhere to. Like all worthwhile pursuits, they take practice, consistency, and effort. But above all, they take the power of God. Just like the lights in our homes, we can't function if we are disconnected from the power source.

"Where there's smoke, there's fire" is a quote often used to highlight the validity of a rumor or to draw attention to someone's unfortunate missteps in life. It's used to reference someone who has fallen victim to the lifestyle of sex, drugs, and rock-and-roll. It's basically an "I told you so".

What if we could shift this paradigm?

What if, when we heard the phrase, "Where there's smoke, there's fire", it was because our lives were burning so brightly with hope and love that people couldn't help but take notice. What if they had to know where this light is coming from? What if they had to follow to see where it was going?

I hope this is one instance you dare to play with fire – to feel the heat of the flame. This burn is a good one –

a refining one. It will allow you to discover, to grow and move toward becoming the person you were created to be. The sparks you throw will cause others to ignite and burn with the same hope and life.

# 8

# HOT COALS

---

I absolutely love coffee. I know we throw the word love around very loosely nowadays. I love that TV show; I love that restaurant; I love my new car, blah, blah, blah. Most of the things we profess our undying adoration and "love" for, are in all reality things we could survive just fine without. The world would keep spinning and the sky would not fall.

Not to say these things aren't important or don't have value, but do we truly love them? With all of this being said, yeah, I still love coffee.

My love for the delicious nectar of the coffee bean has deep-rooted origins in the role it has played in my family.

Coffee has always been like the warm hug of a towel straight out of the dryer after you've been playing outside in the snow so long you can't feel your fingers in your gloves anymore. It is comfort, safety and serenity all wrapped up in one piping hot cup.

I remember going to my grandparents' house and having coffee with my Paw Paw Raby (sugar, milk, and coffee – in that order). It was an innocent time to just hang out – to get to know each other. There was no agenda. It was a time for building relationship. My drink order has changed over the years but the meaning behind my love of the coffee bean has remained unchanged.

---

SIDEBAR: I will only drink "leaded" coffee. No "unleaded" (decaf) for my cup! Decaf is just brown water according to my Paw Paw Raby. I'm positive he will have a cup waiting for me when I see him in Heaven someday.

---

Coffee has been and still is one of the most important materials in building the foundation of my family. It has a way of breaking down walls. It has a strange way of creating life in our family (aside from the caffeine buzz). We have laughed and cried over coffee and sometimes those tears have landed in our cups. But we have always been stronger because of the foundation being built during those times.

Building the foundation is the most crucial part of the

building process. It can also be the longest; painstaking and tedious. Measuring, leveling, and clearing the area to make sure it is free from anything that could cause obstruction or cracks in the future.

If the foundation has been attended to with care, once the building is ready to be erected, the structure is much more likely to stand the test of time. Storms will come and earthquakes will shake (real and metaphorical). A strong foundation is the basis for strength.

It's the same concept when you are building a fire. If you don't build a good pile of hot coals (the foundation), the odds that the fire will continue to burn are slim. Arrange the kindling – a good foundation – then as you add more substantial pieces of wood to the fire, it will continue to burn – hotter and longer.

Maybe this is why so many marriages end in divorce – in Non-Christians and Christians alike. I am one of these statistics. We are so ready to build or buy the house, start the family and build what we are told is the "ideal" life (it looks great on Instagram), that we forget that building the foundation is the most important part. We are trying to build the walls before the foundation is complete.

---

[11] *For no one can lay any foundation other than the one we already have—Jesus Christ.*[12] *Anyone who builds on that foundation may use a variety of materials—gold, silver, jewels, wood, hay, or straw.* [13] *But on the judgment day, fire will reveal*

*what kind of work each builder has done. The fire will show if a person's work has any value. [14] If the work survives, that builder will receive a reward. [15] But if the work is burned up, the builder will suffer great loss. The builder will be saved, but like someone barely escaping through a wall of flames. (1 Corinthians 3:11-15)*

We may or may not be using the wrong materials. But we are trying to rush the process and skipping steps that are crucial along the way.

We need a sense of companionship instead of competition in our relationships. This will allow us to speak to and correct each other, when it is appropriate. It also allows us to receive correction without a sense of defensiveness when given. It allows us to add value to the lives of those around us. I'm still a work in progress here and the mortar is still setting.

For most of my life, I viewed correction as a sign that I had done something wrong. I perceived it as making a good or bad choice. If I was corrected, it was because I thought I was wrong. I didn't see the value of the lesson being taught. Looking back, most of this was just that, my perception. This was the case in school, athletics, at home and even in my marriage. What I have been learning though, is that correction, when given in love can be empowering. It can drive us toward growing into the person that we have the potential of becoming.

Being able to give and receive correction in a

relationship built on a solid foundation is one of the ultimate signs of love. It is about building each other up through love, not tearing each other down by reprimand. It is about letting God incinerate our pride and replace it with His perfect love. Jesus corrects and teaches us because He loves us. How we receive His correction and guidance is a sign of how strong our foundation is. If our walls are built on Jesus, they may get shaken but they will never fall.

# 9

# FIRE GOOD, FIRE BAD

---

*"Fire can be both good and bad. If it's in your furnace, it will keep your house warm. If it's in your attic, it will burn your house down."*

When I heard these words during a conversation, my dad and I were having, it sent a shock wave straight to my soul.

"Wow", I exclaimed.

I immediately thought how this analogy was so all-encompassing and for me, life altering. My mind shifted into overdrive, which when it is running in 6th gear already, can be dangerous. Especially when I'm the one behind the wheel!

What is the significance of the furnace and the attic?

The furnace provides heat to your home. It can keep your pipes from freezing. A warm home can feel inviting, but a cold home makes you shiver and looking for extra layers of blankets for protection from the bitter cold.

The attic is where we store the things that are out of season, we've outgrown, or we want to hide. These are things that we'd rather just forget about or that we try to ignore.

Once we are aware of these things, we can ask God how He wants to work in our hearts. We can let him become the heart arsonist in our life He wants to be. Stop reading for a second and take time to think about and answer the following questions, which have been on repeat in my mind and heart as of late. I invite you to put them on your playlist as well.

*What do I have stored in my attic?* We all have things stored there, but are we willing to engage with them?

*How do I stop the fire in the attic before it consumes everything around it?*

*How do I keep the fire in the furnace burning hot to keep the house warm?*

Even if our furnace is turned up and providing heat, we still need to make sure the heat isn't escaping through the cracks. Check under the doors. Check around the windows. Sometimes we overlook the small areas. The areas we don't always see can be the most crucial. Those areas could be letting valuable heat escape and the cold creep in.

This principle was driven home with me recently when I went to change the filter on my HVAC. The bitter chill of winter was slowly leaving and the heat of the Sacramento summer was coming early (103 in May). I knew I needed to change the filter so I went out to the garage to take care of the small job. When I stepped into the closet I noticed that it was a much colder than it should be. I ran my hand up the side of the plenum and noticed that one side had come apart and was allowing the air to escape into the small closet instead of forcing it into the house. I have no idea how long this crack had been there, but my suspicion is for quite a while since the heat output had been a little sub par as well. A little HVAC tape and about 10 minutes of work and the layer of insulation and protection was fixed.

We need to make sure that our home (our heart) is insulated. Unless we have that layer of protection, even the heat produced by our furnace will be lost through the cracks. It won't be as effective as it should be. Prayer and the power of the Holy Spirit are that insulation. He will give us the reports from the inspection, showing us the areas needing repair, but we are responsible for doing our part to make sure the cracks get sealed. It's a joint effort.

Over the past few years I've realized that there were a lot of things hidden in my attic that weren't beneficial in the journey of becoming the person God created me to be. Some of the things I had tucked away had been there so long that I had to brush away the dust and cobwebs before I could clean house.

Some things I had hidden because I didn't want anyone to know about them. My attic had become congested. It was more than just a fire hazard. It could have burned my life to the ground.

When I was younger, I had a pretty short fuse. It didn't take much for me to get irritated or angry, and I didn't hide it well (more on that later). I realized after becoming a dad, that those behaviors started to slowly creep back in. I was better at hiding them this time (I thought). This wasn't very beneficial. To me or those around me. If I didn't purposefully ask God to change this in my heart and make me more like him, who knows what the effects could've been. I still ask God to change me daily, because i know that He is my strength, even when I am weak.

What I've been learning over that same time is that my furnace – the thing that provides heat to my home – is my heart. There were a lot of cracks that needed sealing. I was letting a lot of heat escape and a lot of cold seep in. Proverbs 4:23 tells us, *"guard your heart above all else, for it determines the course of your life".*

Are the things I'm watching, the things I'm listening to, the people I hang around, and the way I'm conducting my self in my relationships fueling my heart? Are they pressing me to be more like Jesus? Are they adding fuel to the furnace of my heart so I burn brighter, love more extravagantly and serve others without thinking about what I get in return?

This is a tall order for most of us when we examine how we are fueling our hearts; it continues to be for me. I have to live in constant awareness of what I allow to penetrate my heart – what I allow to take root. This doesn't mean we have to withdraw from everyone and lock ourselves in our room to stay away from the things that aren't nurturing and developing our heart. It is a call to be aware and mindful of what we allow to influence us.

## 10

# TRICKLE DOWN

———

Our thoughts are like fertilizer to our hearts. What we consistently and deliberately think about *will* trickle down into our hearts. The more we water those thoughts, the more those roots will spread and take hold; positive or negative.

What begins as a thought – a seed, will put down roots in our hearts. What takes root in our heart will spread to the world around us. What we focus our minds on will become the posture of our hearts.

We have two choices.

Feed and water them with truth and life.

Feed and water them with negativity and death.

———

Use your words to build up; not to tear down (yourself and others).

So many times, we hit our knees out of desperation. We come to God with our pleas for peace during the storms of life. The reality of the matter is that God is here and He hears us. He wants to give us the things we so desperately need. When our thoughts have us spiraling into a cyclone of turmoil, we cry out for peace.

I've done this so many times.

*I wanted peace and calm for my anxious thoughts while going through a divorce.*

But if it was a good day, my thoughts usually weren't focused on the Father.

*I wanted peace to calm the fear of being alone.*

But when I was around friends and family, I usually wasn't very thankful for their company and support.

*I wanted peace in the midst of looking for a job on the other side of the country.*

But I wasn't thankful for the ones I found or the fact I could apply for them online from 2300 miles away.

*I wanted to be free of an addiction to pornography.*

But when I was walking in freedom, I was quick to forget that the Holy Spirit is the one who freed me.

My thought process and my focus (more on that shortly) were not always what they needed to be. Because of where I focused my thoughts, the posture of my heart was off center. It wasn't at peace. Peace is a natural side effect of walking in the Spirit. It's not something we have to have to chase down. Where we focus our thoughts *will* direct the posture of our hearts. And the posture of our hearts will determine the course of our life.

---

*And now, dear brothers and sisters, one final thing. Fix your thoughts on what is true, and honorable, and right, and pure, and lovely, and admirable. Think about things that are excellent and worthy of praise. (Philippians 4:8)*

---

A heart of praise, gratitude and thankfulness is where we need to be – day in and day out. When these things flow out of us, the peace that passes all understanding will flow into us. That peace has ripple effects that will move those around us. That peace is alive and active. This is one way we can *be* the Gospel to those around every day.

# 11

# ADJUST YOUR FOCUS

When it comes to going to the doctor, I can be very stubborn. I don't know if this is a typical "guy thing" (whatever that means) or if it's just a trait I inherited from my Grandpas. I knew I couldn't see as well as I used to, but I didn't want to break down and go. But since my eyes had gotten progressively worse, I decided to make a change. So, at the urging of my wife (she was right), after being a terrible patient for about 15 years, I gave in and scheduled an appointment with the optometrist.

What I found out amazed me. The culprit for my obscured vision was that I had an astigmatism in both eyes.

After my initial exam, the doctor started changing the lens filters on her equipment, asking me to read line after line on the eye chart, until we found the ones that corrected my field of vision. Once things came into focus, there was a sense of sharpness and clarity that hadn't been there in quite a while. Why did I wait so long to make this change?

Our hearts and how we love are much like our eyes. Sometimes they become blurry and out of focus. Without routine checkups, we might not know there is an issue that needs addressed – that we need new lenses. If we don't know there is correction needed, we may never get the prescription that could set things straight. If I hadn't listened to my wife and went to the optometrist, I may never have gotten the prescription so I could see the way I needed to. I was missing a lot of the beauty around me and only seeing a blurred version of the truth.

This happens when we view our world with a blurry set of lenses.

So many people these days are looking for validation by how many views, likes, shares their posts or insanely edited pictures receive. How many "friends" or "followers" do we have? We let our focus get blurred from what is truly important in life.

Instead we should ask:

"Who and what are we following?"

"Are these people or things helping us grow into the people we were created to be?"

"What is the motivation behind what we're posting?"

These tools are not inherently bad. In fact, they can be very beneficial and helpful. But when our focus and identity become tied to them, it becomes a slippery slope.

It seems however, that our online interaction is quickly trumping our uninterrupted human interaction. Me too. Guilty as charged. It's a strange way of seeking validation.

As soon as we see the notification that someone has double clicked our picture on Instagram or pressed like on Facebook, a tidal wave of endorphins floods our brains. But just as quickly as the waves come, they recede. It's a vicious cycle.

If our life and priorities are out of focus, our perspective will be blurry. If we have a disordered love, we have not fully submitted to a life lived wholly for the glory of God our Father.

Is there anything in our lives we value more than our relationship with Jesus? If so, it needs to be put in its place. If anything is placed above Jesus in our life, we need to adjust our focus. Our lens needs to be changed.

When I adjust the focus of this relationship first, it begins to sharpen the focus of my marriage as well. I see my relationship with my children more clearly. Everything comes into focus when I'm wearing the right set of lenses.

<u>KNOW THIS</u>: Jesus loves you – relentlessly, passionately and without fail.

Today, let's all try to find and acknowledge the value in ourselves and those around us. When we adjust the focus of the lens through which we see the world, our entire perspective will start to change.

# 12

# GRATITUDE IS LIKE GASOLINE

---

I can hear the warm hum of the alarm clock on my phone going off on the bedside table. It is doing its best to coax me back into the land of the living. It's another 4 am wake-up call—time to head to work. I'm fighting back with everything inside of me.

"Are you kidding me", I say out loud.

Some mornings, I wonder what I'm doing folding gym towels and cleaning exercise equipment. "I have a Master's Degree", I spout off.

Even though I've been doing this for a long time now,

my head still questions why I should be awake at such an insane time of the day.

Then suddenly my heart, like a defenseman, slams me into the boards. "Stay faithful in the small things. Respect the process. Give your best in everything you do. Even when it's tough. Remember, it matters".

For nine months, these early morning sucker punches were daily reminders of the reason I do what I do. First, to take care of my family. But also to serve the people in my organization and our clients the best I can. With that, my heart shifts to a posture of gratitude.

Gratitude is powerful. Gratitude has a way of transforming our hearts. Gratitude changes our "have to" into "get to".

This fundamental truth has infected my DNA to a degree I never expected over the past several years. I know none of us have ever been grateful for an infection, but this is one I hope I am never cured from.

You see gratitude is like gasoline to a fire. When you soak your heart in gratitude, your attitude, your passions, and your purpose – the things that make you tick – take on a new meaning. The roaring wildfire that ignites can be uncontrollable.

Living in Northern California during a severe drought, there has been no escaping the reality and devastation of wildfires. They've consumed tens of thousands of acres of forest. They've consumed homes and in some cases, ravaged entire communities.

What if our hearts, when lit on fire and burning uncontrollably with gratitude, consumed and overtook our homes and communities? What would this look like? Could this fire be the remedy to the drought of hopelessness that has plagued our world? Will you strike a match with me and watch the spark of gratitude spread?

Gratitude is the foundation for good posture in life. This posture, whether physical, mental, spiritual, or relational is the vehicle that can cause you to thrive. Or it can cause you to break down along the side of the road waiting for the tow truck to haul you in. Unless we have a heart that has been healed and is grateful, I am convinced that we will never be fully able to live the life that God created us to live.

As I stated earlier, when we have a strong foundation, everything built on top of it will be stronger. My friend and one of the world's leading expert on gratitude, Dr. Robert Emmons has spent years studying the far-reaching effects of gratitude. Here is what he has to say:

―――――――

*Gratitude has two components. First, it's an affirmation of goodness. We affirm that there are good things in the world, gifts and benefits we've received. This doesn't mean life is perfect; it doesn't ignore complaints, burdens, and hassles. But when we look at life as a whole, gratitude encourages us to identify some amount of goodness in our life.*

*The second part of gratitude is figuring out where that*

*goodness comes from. We recognize the sources of this goodness as being outside of ourselves. It didn't stem from anything we necessarily did ourselves in which we might take pride. We can appreciate positive traits in ourselves, but I think true gratitude involves a humble dependence on others: we acknowledge that other people—or even higher powers, if you're of a spiritual mindset—gave us many gifts, big and small, to help us achieve the goodness in our lives[1].*

It is easy for most of us to hide and live life in the shadows; the places and mindsets that tell us to take the easy road. It's easy to complain. Most of us, myself included, can do it without even thinking.

To move toward and live a life of substance, we need to embrace a heart posture of gratitude.

It takes *work*.

It takes *effort*.

It takes *consistency*.

But as we do this, we see that even when we encounter storms in life, the anchor of hope tethered by gratitude, will not let us drift.

I love how the Message version of the Bible puts it.

*My counsel for you is simple and straightforward: Just go ahead with what you've been given. You received Christ Jesus, the Master; now live him. You're deeply rooted in him. You're well-*

---

*constructed upon him. You know your way around the faith. Now do what you've been taught. School's out; quit studying the subject and start living it! And let your living spill over into thanksgiving. (Colossians 2:6-7 MSG)*

Here's where to start:

1. <u>Write down 3-4 things each day you are grateful for</u>: This is a great way to start reframing our mindset and our focus. Set aside a specific time for this (very important). Unless we make this time a priority, it is easy to let it fall off the grid when the busyness of life presses in. As this practice becomes more consistent, you may see your list grow.

2. <u>Start with the easy ones</u>: Your family, health, your home, etc. But don't stop there. Dig in and examine what you are really grateful . Here is one example from my journal: *I am grateful for the failures in my life. Each one of them has taught me a lesson and helped me learn and grow into the person I am in the process of becoming.*

3. <u>Be consistent</u>:This is key! Practice may not make us perfect, but it does makes us proficient. The magic is in the process, not the product.

4. <u>Read each one, out loud and with conviction</u>: There is power in our words. When we boldly declare these areas of gratefulness out loud and on a daily basis, we change our beliefs and the surrounding atmosphere.

If we learn to be truly grateful, we will treat failure and success the same: *WITH THANKS!*

Today, will you choose to live your life with a posture of gratitude?

Let's commit, together to *repeating this out loud* to start each day:

*I will live my life with a posture and heart of GRATITUDE.*

Let's commit, together to *declaring this over ourselves* to start each day:

*I will live my life with a posture and heart of GRATITUDE.*

## 13

# BE INTENTIONAL

---

When I was younger, my dad would set apart a special day for me and each of my brothers where the focus was 100% on us. The great thing about these days was that there was no agenda, no place we had to be and no distractions. Whatever we wanted to do, wherever we wanted to go, we did. They usually consisted of a video arcade and McDonald's, but the intentional nature of our dad sowing his love, attention, and the importance of being present and engaged in our lives, is etched into each of our hearts.

I loved "Joey Raby Day" and thought for a while it should be a National holiday. I still love the times when my dad and I get to spend an uninterrupted, no agenda day together. Even though we live on opposite sides of the country, the imprint is still there.

Those days had such an impact on me that Michelle and I do these now with our kids. We want them to know no matter how busy life can be, we always have time for them. Time to intentionally focus on fueling their hearts. We want them know we value and love them. Not because of what they do, but because of who they are. When we take this deliberate time with each of them we can see a change in their behavior. We can see a change in their attitude. They have a sense of peace in them which can be lost when the winds of a chaotic life are swirling. And I'm sure the toys and candy they sometimes get doesn't hurt either.

Just like the controlled burns we talked about earlier, farmers have to be intentional when they plant as well. They have to be diligent with the process. We have to sow if we ever want to see a harvest – in our friendships, our marriages, our homes and our businesses. Where we sow the seeds may be up to us, but whether they take root and the type of crop they yield many times isn't up to us. We can't get too wrapped up in the harvest but we *must* be intentional about the planting.

Listen to the words written in Luke 8:5-8.

---

*"A farmer went out to plant his seed. As he scattered it across his field, some seed fell on a footpath where it was stepped on,*

*and the birds ate it. 6 Other seed fell among rocks. It began to grow, but the plant soon wilted and died for lack of moisture. 7 Other seed fell among thorns that grew up with it and choked out the tender plants. 8 Still other seed fell on fertile soil. This seed grew and produced a crop that was a hundred times as much as had been planted!" (Luke 8:5-8)*

We will have an impact by living our lives every day knowing we are loved by our Creator. When we let His love for us and our love for Him pour out onto every person that we meet, even the bleakest of circumstances are being cultivated for change.

Sometimes it may feel like our glass is almost empty, but when our reservoir is in Him, we will never run dry. We are vessels. Before He can fill us, we have to empty ourselves.

When we empty ourselves—of our pride, our agendas, our prejudices –anything that is not glorifying to Him, God will fill us with the power and hope that only He can give. But we have to surrender.

Something is only as valuable as what someone will pay for it. Jesus gave His life so we would be saved. This means we are a part of the most valuable transaction ever to take place. Our value lies in who we are, not what we do or have done. It's about what Christ did for us. It's about who we are becoming. Not about what we post to our social media feed (filtered or not).

Sometimes I wonder if I am insulting God by not

valuing myself the way He values me. He paid for me with His life. Am I willing to live for Him with mine?

My value doesn't lie in the words I'm typing here. It's not tied to the number of people that read, like or purchase this book. My value lies in the fact that I was created on purpose and for a purpose. I am fearfully and wonderfully made. I am His child.

I wish this is something I would have realized and believed earlier in life. How many years did I waste chasing wishing wells, but not using the water from the well to water the seeds that were being sown into my heart?

Don't throw your dreams in the wishing well. They will hit the bottom of that dark cavern and you may never see them again. Instead, plant them in deep rich soil and every day water them, tend to them. Bathe them in the sunlight. Don't leave your life or the lives of those around you to chance.

You may have to pull out some weeds and fight off intruders who are trying to eat and destroy your crop before it's ready. You may not harvest overnight. In time however, with patience and persistence, what you yield will be more than you could ever imagine. Be faithful with small things. Wait and see what happens.

We can't hope but not work.

We have to grind just a little more today than we did yesterday.

Every day we have an opportunity to grow or sit stuck in the mud.

We can wait but we still have to work.

We can practice or we can pout.

We can either find a way to solve our problems or we can let our problems overtake us.

God chose you.

God chose me.

We have the power to choose if we want to live a life of impact. But we have to be intentional about it. Reckless love is the fuel. Reckless love will start the fire. We have to keep it burning. God has given us the tools. But we get to choose to use them or not.

I'm worth it.

You're worth it.

We are worth it.

The choice is mine.

The choice is yours.

## 14

# PASSION & PURPOSE

———————

Driving back from South Lake Tahoe, some friends and I mistakenly took a different road coming back than on the way up (I swear I knew where I was going). What we saw on this inadvertent detour blew my mind. We saw hundreds, if not thousands of trees that had been destroyed by flames in one on the many wildfires that have ravaged Northern California over the past several years during the drought.

I had seen the news stories and read about them online, but seeing the devastation in person changed my perspective. It made me think about what happens when we let our passion be the principal driver in our lives.

When we live controlled by our passions and emotions, if we aren't careful, we can leave a barren forest of friends and relationships in our wake; devoid of life-giving vegetation.

We need others in our life. If we aren't careful, we can let the unbridled flames of passion lay waste to one of the most important resources we have – community.

We've all heard the rally cry. Follow your passion! In the middle of a thunder of clapping hands and epic cheers this always sounds good and gets us "fired up". Does it create lasting change in our lives or the lives of those around us though? Or is it merely motivation's version of a "get rich quick" scheme?

There's a difference between living fueled by passion and living controlled by passion.

Passion is based on emotion.

Passion is mobile. It can change with time.

Passion can be selfish. It is "me" focused.

Passion can and will deceive the heart.

Passion is only a spark.

We have to keep passion in its place.

We can't let it run wild and unbridled. If it's not watched or tended to, it can be very dangerous.

Stallions have to be tamed to be truly used for their purpose. There is a fine line between breaking their will and taming their will. Like an untamed stallion, passion can change direction – often without warning or reason. When we act on our passions without first filtering them through the lens of prayer and the power of the Holy Spirit, we set ourselves up for misguided pursuits. We have to let Jesus tame our hearts in order for us to fulfill the purpose He has for our lives.

Just because we are passionate about something doesn't mean it is our purpose. Passion is only the first piece of the equation.

Purpose, on the other hand is a different animal. Purpose is the "X" factor. Purpose is the unquenchable fire in our belly that cannot be contained – only shared. Unless our hearts are truly set on fire and burning continuously, we will never experience true and lasting change—true and lasting joy.

Purpose flows from the heart (the wellspring of life).

Purpose is what we believe deep in the core of our being.

Purpose is why we wake up.

Why we breathe.

Why we fight.

Why we hustle.

Purpose is always "others" focused.

Purpose is an uncontrollable fire.

Passion may be the spark that starts a fire inside of us but purpose is the fuel that keeps it burning.

Purpose is a about adding value to others' lives, even when they may not see it in themselves.

Purpose is about doing and living out what sets your soul ablaze. It's about wanting to leave the world a better place for those who come after us. It's about giving of the time, resources, and unique gifts we all have.

On one occasion, Jesus had to diffuse some serious tension when the mother of two of the disciples asked if her boys could sit at His left and right when they got to Heaven (Matthew 20:21). I mean, can you imagine? Did they send her to ask? Or did she go on her own? I'm a bit of a mamma's boy but, come on fellas!

Jesus wasted no time in diffusing the frustration of the group. What he said tells us so much, not only about what His mission and purpose was, but how he would accomplish it.

---

*But among you it will be different. Whoever wants to be a leader among you must be your servant, and whoever wants to be first among you must become your slave. Jesus' purpose was to serve. He did that by laying down His life. He knew His purpose and everything He did (as the Father told Him) was about fulfilling it. He was intentional in how He served.*
*(Matthew 20:26-27).*

---

*What is my unique purpose?*

*What am I doing to put wood on that fire to keep it burning?*

We can have many passions. But we can have only one purpose. Purpose comes from a heart posture of serving.

Purpose is about adding value to another life while adding value to our own life. It is about being a good steward with the things God has given so we can be a blessing to others.

15

# WHY WE NEED COMMUNITY

---

Growing up in a small town, we knew virtually everyone. It wasn't uncommon to find someone taking a nap on the couch in between classes or rifling through one of the refrigerators (feeding 4 boys and an army of friends requires stock piling). It wasn't uncommon for someone to drop by – if they needed help or just wanted to hang out and say hi. This is the home that I grew up in and the foundational community that I got to be a part of.

My parents were very adamant about building and maintaining relationships–about establishing community.

I'm very thankful for this.

Even though we know the importance of surrounding

ourselves with people and thriving in a healthy community, we still go through periods of loneliness and isolation.

Have you ever heard someone make the statement, "I feel like I'm all alone in a crowded room?"

Have you ever been the one to say this? To be honest, I've heard myself say this more than a few times in my life.

People today seem to be growing more experience-rich, but at the same time becoming increasingly relationship-poor.

An ever-growing number of our "personal" interactions come from behind the interface of a screen (smartphone, tablet, and computer). They can rob us of one of our most basic human needs—to truly be loved and accepted by a real community. They have a way of turning us into ghosts in the midst of a sea of people.

This is true in our daily lives, our schools, our businesses and sadly in many cases our churches and families. What would happen if we spent more time intentionally focused on building relationships and getting to know the people we are serving, the people in our communities and even those in our own home? I believe that we would see our connections, our marriages and possibly even our revenues (in business) grow exponentially. That is a return on investment that would benefit us all!

We all have an inherent desire to belong—to feel loved and welcome—to feel safe. There is no better way to experience this than in a healthy community; a community in which we can be us—authentically and truthfully.

No acting.

No pretense.

No performance.

Intentionally investing time and effort into building this pillar of our lives can drastically change the joy that we experience every day. It's not always easy though. At times it may mean cutting people out of your life who are holding you back from becoming who you were created to be. The people who don't believe in you now, are the same people who will someday be telling others how they know you. This controlled burn will allow you to get rid of the underbrush so that the greatness that is inside of you can grow and flourish.

Intentionally investing in the gift of community also means embracing those around you by speaking life into and pouring love into those that you do life with, day in and day out.

Love is the most sought after and valuable currency in the world. The amazing thing is that when we hold onto it like we will lose it, it doesn't grow. The only way to gain interest is to give love away. This is how we grow rich in life.

Life is meant to be lived in relationship—in community. God is a community in and of himself.

God the Father

Jesus the Son

The Holy Spirit

We can thrive in a healthy community as the people God created each of us to be. This is a place where your story, your heartbeat, your fingerprint and your DNA makes you 100% unique. When all of our stories are told together, it forms the most angelic choir you could ever imagine. When all of those hearts beat together at once, when gratitude is expressed en masse, when love is given authentically, it creates a thunder so loud that it reverberates to even the most desolate and lonely places.

We all need community.

We all need love. We all need each other.

We all need Jesus.

Let's venture together to take back the idea of real community that has started to erode.

Real, true, honest community is a force to be reckoned with.

Let's change the paradigm.

Let's shift our culture........ together.

## 16

# HOSTAGE NEGOTIATION

———

*"Often the words we speak are only part of the conversation we're having. The real conversation is about whether or not we think the person we're talking to is worth listening to or important. And if we can communicate that, and nothing else, we are communicating something enormous and validating." – Donald Miller*

Some things in life you can never be prepared for. Marriage and being a parent are two those things.

I've always thought I was pretty good listener and communicator. When Michelle and I got married, I had a sneaking suspicion that this might not be the case. It didn't take long for my suspicion to be confirmed. Imagine my surprise when we had one of our first big fights and I didn't win! For the record, winning an argument in marriage should never be a mission – resolution should be. Our aim should be to try and out-serve one another, not out-argue. One makes an enemy; the other makes an ally.

I learned that I only listened enough to calculate my rebuttal to whatever Michelle was saying. What I thought was good communication really just meant that I liked to hear myself talk (I'm still a work in progress).

I've gotten remarkable at talking during the first 37 years of my life (maybe I missed my call as a lawyer). What I find more and more is that this is not always a good trait – for my marriage, my friendships or my relationship with Jesus.

Too many times, I've let my mouth move faster than a super charged muscle car. The things that come screaming out sound better in the crowded and often overly busy space in my brain. They sometimes don't come out encouraging or valuable to those who hear them. And they can come at the most inopportune times.

Our parents taught my brothers and me this at an early age, in what we were convinced was an attempt to get us to be nicer to one another. What I didn't realize was they were teaching us a valuable lesson for later in life. The words of the following verse provide a blueprint to follow if you fall into this category like I many times do.

———

*"My dear brothers and sisters, take note of this: Everyone should*

*be quick to listen, slow to speak and slow to become angry."*
*(James 1:9)*

---

We have all been held hostage at some point in our lives to beliefs, practices, or mindsets that are damaging to our relationships. I'm convinced that our sense of real and edifying communication is just one area that has been taken hostage.

If I'm constantly talking, it's difficult if not impossible to hear God's or anyone else's voice in my life. It's only a matter of time before I insert my foot into my mouth.

These are just a few principles that the Lord has been teaching me (I'm learning):

1. <u>Don't be eager to share your opinion</u>: Be patient. Actually listen.

2. <u>Try to put yourself in the other person's situation</u>: How would it make me feel? How would I react? How would I want others to respond? If an individual is vulnerable enough to share their heart and soul with you, treat it with care. A heart can be the most fragile thing on the planet in one moment, but the hardest the next. The direction that a heart goes is greatly influenced by how it's treated.

3. <u>Give grace</u>: If we are in the habit of compartmentalizing the grace we give, those around us will get into the habit of compartmentalizing the love they share with us. Radical grace is the driver of

radical love. Grace in its nature is undeserved, but that doesn't give us the right to withhold it from others. Jesus doesn't withhold grace from us. We need to follow His example.

The only way to truly be free from the things that hold us hostage is through the power of the Holy Spirit and through Jesus Christ the son. It is not about damage control. It's about freedom. Like the quote at the beginning of the chapter says, "*The real conversation is about whether or not we think the person we're talking to is worth listening to or important.*"

Real love thrives with the presence of conversation and the absence of condemnation.

Do we value what the Holy Spirit has been telling us?

I sure hope so.

He is always speaking, but too many times we can't hear him because of all the noise in our lives. I'm beginning to think I might be a recovering extrovert. I love to be around people. This was woven into the fabric of my DNA at an early age. But the older I get, I'm valuing the silence and times of appropriate unavailability just as much, if not more. These times give me a chance to stop talking and become more actively engaged in listening.

To God.

To my wife.

To my kids.

To others in my life.

When we were younger, we learned that if we were on fire we should STOP, DROP and ROLL. As I've gotten older, I've found that we need to STOP, LISTEN, and FOLLOW what the Holy Spirit is telling us if we want to *catch fire*!

Jesus was sent as our advocate – our hostage negotiator. He came as a ransom for us so that we can be free from bondage and live a life of freedom. The same Spirit that raised Christ from the dead is alive and living in each of us as believers. If I want to tune my heart into the beat of the Father's, I need to give him space to speak.

<u>*Moral of the story*</u> – sometimes, I just need to slow down, shut up and listen.

## 17

# THE GATEWAY

———————

Addiction is a strange and powerful thing. It is not selective. It will try to come for all of us in some way, shape, or form. Sometimes it uses guerrilla warfare, while other times its tactics are more subtle. I've faced my challenges and struggles and I didn't always come out on the winning side when the bell rang. It took a long time for me to realize that I could never have victory when I was the one trying to throw the punches. It still takes daily training to make sure I am in the shape required to fight if and when the next flurry of punches from the enemy comes.

I needed more than someone just in my corner coaching

me. I needed someone to fight alongside me – someone who has already won the battle. That someone is Jesus. I've never seen a fighter go into a fight all by themselves. They have an entourage in their corner – a support system. Why would I approach the struggles of life any differently?

It seems that around every corner there is a story of someone falling into addiction before they realized it. It starts with something small – an introduction – a gateway. Before long, they are wondering how they reached the point where they get backed into a corner.

I'm convinced kindness is a gateway. Sometimes the smallest act, an encouraging word – a specific and sincere compliment, can open the floodgates for so much more. People are more likely to respond to kindness than condemnation. Kindness in the face of adversity is the gateway to the miraculous. Jesus wants us to react with kindness. Is there a simpler way to being serving those around us than just being kind?

When I was in my early 20s, I thought I was a pretty cool guy. What I realized one night when my wife insisted on watching a batch of dreaded home movies changed my perspective and my heart very quickly. To be honest, it felt like someone stuck me with a Taser. The shock I felt was excruciating.

My little brother Jonathan and I are almost 11 years apart so growing up we didn't have many things in common. Most times I just saw him as the annoying little brother. As I said earlier, I had dreams at one point of becoming a famous musician. During this time, I let the small-town notoriety go to my head.

In the movie, Jonathan was giving a tour of my parents' house with an old RCA camcorder (pre iPhone), walking from room to room and around the rest of the property, giving color commentary like a 10-year-old field reporter on location. My band mates and I were loading our gear into the van for a show that night. Watching as he came up to me while I was sitting on the kitchen counter to "interview" me was the moment I got hit with the Taser (figuratively).

The look on my face as he spoke was more piercing than daggers. It was more like a scud missile.

"How dare you talk to me", shot from his eyes.

In that instant, watching the scene replay on the TV, something clicked in my heart. My little brother was doing what a little brother does – wanting to talk to his big brother. I thought about how my actions and words must have made him feel. It made me sick to my stomach. I had to do more than apologize. I had to change. Since then, our relationship has grown extremely close. He actually helped me design the cover of this book. He is an amazing brother, husband, father and business man (if you live in the Franklin/Williamson county area of Southern Illinois, go to Burg's Hair Parlor in West Frankfort. Ask for Jonathan. You won't be disappointed).

You see, once kindness is injected into our veins, it can have a systemic effect. It is an inescapable high that can cause a contact buzz to those on both ends of the transaction. It will infect our neural pathways. It will infect the way we think about and view others. It will infect and overtake our hearts. It will cause that fire to spread in every area of our lives:

In our marriages.

In our families.

In our churches.

In our neighborhoods.

It will overtake our communities and our world.

When others see we genuinely care about them and we have no agenda, they will feel the love of Jesus flowing from us. As I stated earlier, love will open doors that ambition never could.

I have never heard anyone say they are a recovering kindness addict.

Well, I want to be an addict. And I hope I never recover.

# 18

# STOP SHOOTING AT
# YOURSELF

———

I remember one evening after moving to Sacramento I was sitting in my living room scrolling through Facebook. I noticed a post from a friend of mine I had known since grade school. I hadn't seen or heard from him since we graduated high school. Suddenly, I felt an overwhelming sense that I needed to reach out to him and another old friend to ask them to forgive me. As we got older, and our friend groups changed from that of the small-town school we grew up in, I began to treat them poorly. They didn't deserve this, and I needed to ask their forgiveness.

To my surprise, one of them actually responded. I didn't expect it. A sense of relief, like a weight being lifted from my shoulders, washed over me. Not because he accepted my apology, but because I was obedient to what I needed to do. It wasn't easy, but it was necessary. That area of the past didn't have a hold on my heart anymore. These words healed. They brought life. Each time we forgive, we take back ground where our joy has been stolen. The more we forgive, the closer we come to sinking the battleship of regret and bitterness.

---

*The tongue can bring life or death. Those who love to talk will reap the consequences. (Proverbs 18:21).*

---

I believe this is true. Most times when we hear this though, we assume that it is about how what we say to another person affects their reality. An unexpected compliment can send us on a euphoria trip that is hard to rival. On the other side of that coin, we can all probably remember how the cutting words of another made us feel lower than we can ever imagine.

I remember one instance where a coach of mine unleashed a barrage of heated words at me in front of a gymnasium full of people after fouling out of a junior high basketball game. It shattered my will and in that moment crippled my belief in myself.

I would assert that the power of our words to either

---

build up or destroy is equally important to remember when we are talking to ourselves. We can fire words of negativity with silver bullet accuracy, many times without a second thought. It can be like a game of Russian roulette where the chances of landing on an empty chamber are smaller than landing on a loaded one.

We were created on purpose and for a purpose. We have a choice: to encourage or tear down others; to encourage or tear down ourselves.

We can throw bricks or use bandages.

You've heard it said the pen is mightier than the sword. The words from our lips are more deadly than both of them combined. The amazing thing is, the same chamber that houses this power, can also be a receptacle of healing.

Over the years, I've become a deadly sniper when it comes to how I speak to myself. I've always had a sharp tongue and quick wit (these have not always been beneficial). What I didn't realize, was how many times I had turned the barrel on myself. I rarely missed the bulls-eye standing at point blank range. The words of negativity I've fired into my heart have been deadly poison.

The more we fire, the more those words take root in our heart and soul until they infect the DNA of who we believe we are.

I'm not worthy of love.

It's too hard, so I won't try.

I'm not smart enough.

He/She is better looking than me.

Do any of these sound familiar?

I know I have been guilty of this in my life.

But there is hope for redemption and healing.

The power of our words when used constructively, not only has the power to change our perception and belief about who we are, but also to change the atmosphere of the environment we live in. Our home lives, our marriages, and relationships, the places we work and serve and every seemingly small interaction we have, can be drastically altered and affected by the power of our words – to ourselves and to others.

There is an endless stream of voices trying to speak into our lives – some good, some bad. Those little voices sometimes seem to scream louder than anything else in our lives by telling us we're not worthy or we'll never measure up. Maybe those voices are telling us that we'll never weather the storm that life is throwing at us. Whatever those voices are saying, YOU DON'T HAVE TO LISTEN!

The words you choose to speak and listen to are just that – a choice. How you decide to use them will directly impact not only the trajectory of the lives of others, they will impact the trajectory of your own life. What direction do you want to move?

You have the ability and the power to talk to yourself – to declare into and over your life that you are worthy. You are fearfully and wonderfully made. You can weather the storm and find a safe harbor. Remember, a smooth sea never made a skillful sailor. Your anchor is tied to the hope we have in Jesus Christ!

You are unique.

You are valuable and loved.

You can change the world.

You are stronger than you know. Sometimes you just need to challenge yourselves to believe it.

You are a child of God....The Creator the universe.

He loves you infinitely more than you can ever comprehend.

The tongue can bring life or death.

Choose life.

# 19

# \ BRŌ-KƏN\

---

Merriam-Webster defines BROKEN as:

1. Violently separated into parts: shattered
2. Damaged or altered
3. Violated by transgression
4. Being irregular, interrupted, or full of obstacles
5. Made weak or infirm
6. Reduced in rank

Smashed, shattered, fragmented, splintered, crushed, snapped, in pieces, destroyed, defective or ruptured. All of these words are just another way of describing something that has been broken.

I don't know if any of these words describe you, but I can promise you, they do me, at least at certain times in my life. I used to think admitting that I was broken or felt defective, the furthest thing from perfection, was a sign of weakness. In our culture, especially for men, this has been preached, and has sadly been accepted for years.

Don't show weakness.

Don't cry.

Be a man.

Be strong.

Man up.

Don't let them know you're scared.

We need to break this cycle of thinking.

Honestly, sometimes this still isn't easy for me. I'll admit that I'm a bit of a crier (alright a big crier), especially since I've become a husband and a daddy. More times than I can admit, I want to give the perception I'm alright and things are always smooth sailing. To be honest though, this isn't always true. I'm aware and grateful that I've been blessed. But sometimes the storms that this life throws at us toss me around and beat me up. I'm sure many of you could say the same thing.

Why is this the case?

The funny thing is that being broken many times is right where God wants us! It isn't until we are broken that the light can begin to shine in.

*Going through the motions doesn't please you; a flawless performance is nothing to you. I learned God-worship when my pride was shattered. Heart-shattered lives ready for love don't for a moment escape God's notice. (Psalm 51:17 MSG)*

It's OK to be broken, because there is someone who can put us back together.

It's OK to admit it too.

Broken can be beautiful.

It wasn't until I could admit that I am a broken and flawed person that God could take these broken pieces and re-purpose them into a new creation and set my life on a whole new trajectory. He was always able, but I had to be willing to trust Him completely and surrender. He can do the same for you. He wants to do the same for you.

20

# CLEAN-OUT DAYS (WHAT I LEARNED FROM CLEANING OUT MY GARAGE)

———————

Clean-out days come a lot around our house these days. Going through closets, toy boxes, the garage—what haven't we used? What have we outgrown? What has broken? You all know the drill. Some of you are getting antsy just reading this. I'm getting antsy writing this. For most of us, it can be a BIG task!

My wife is the queen of clean-out days. From OfferUp to Craigslist and Facebook Marketplace, if its lifespan has reached the end in our home, she can find it a new one.

She loves the fresh start – a clean template to build something new from. I wouldn't say we are minimalists, but I am starting to see the allure of that lifestyle.

Since we have two very mobile little ones running around the house, whose energy seems to grow every day (and a daddy and mommy whose energy does the opposite) toys break easily and often. Even despite our best efforts to the contrary, it still happens. Most times when we run across these "broken" toys, it's easier to toss them in the garbage than taking the time fix them.

During one of these clean out days, this whole picture got me thinking about what God does when one of His children, His creations break. I don't think God believes in "clean out days" the way we do.

I say this because God doesn't believe in throwing out the "broken toys". God always wants to and will take the time to fix us. He wants to mend us and restore us. He wants to show us He loves us even though we are broken and feel as though we are not of use. We have to be a willing participant in the process though.

Brennan Manning made this statement:

---

*"The Lord does not cherish us as we deserve. If that were the case, we would be desolate—but as He must, unable to do otherwise".*

---

HE IS LOVE.

Wow! This truth hit me in the face like a right cross from a prizefighter. God is LOVE. It sounds simple. It sounds very Sunday school. Sometimes those are the things we need. Sometimes those are the things I need.

God doesn't care about our resume.

God doesn't love us because of what we can (or think we can) do for Him.

God doesn't love us because of what we bring to the table.

God loves us despite what we bring to the table.

God just loves us! Period.

Many times, we see ourselves looking like the Isle of Misfit Toys rather than the perfectly arranged shelves of Macy's (or Wal-Mart) at Christmas time. In the eyes of the Father, we are beautiful. He has a crazy way of taking broken things and turning them into something new.

Who knew I could learn so much by cleaning out the garage!

# 21

# PICKING UP THE PIECES

———

*"Trust in the Lord with all your heart and lean not on your own understanding. In all your ways acknowledge Him and He will direct your paths"* (Proverbs 3:5–6)

I am self-admittedly not very good at putting puzzles together. My wife and both of our kids can put me to shame on this in a heartbeat. To be totally honest, when the box of pieces gets dumped onto the table or the floor, the first thing that pops into my head is "What a mess".

When I get down to attempting to put the pieces into place so it hopefully resembles the picture on the box, I always seem to be missing at least one piece. It always holds me back from seeing the finished product.

Sometimes life feels like that puzzle. We keep trying to put all the pieces together only to end up with missing ones. Or worse yet, we end up trying to make pieces fit where they aren't designed to go.

We work so hard to manipulate circumstances around us but in the end, we watch them unravel. We want things to go according to our plans. I am guilty of this. I want things to be logical. I want them to make sense. However, this verse tells us that our logic is not the same as God's.

---

*"My thoughts are nothing like your thoughts," says the Lord. "And my ways are far beyond anything you could imagine. For just as the heavens are higher than the earth, so my ways are higher than your ways and my thoughts higher than your thoughts." (Isaiah 55:8-9)*

---

God's understanding and love is so far above what our human minds can comprehend on our own. Sometimes, it's hard, if not impossible for us to see the completeness of the big picture. We can only know what we've seen and learned. This is where leaning on God comes in. He is the missing piece to the puzzle of our lives. He's the linchpin. Only he can bring understanding where we lack.

We often think it's easier to start by finding the border pieces first and then working our way in. God, like He always loves to do, flips that idea totally upside down. He wants to start with the pieces on the inside and work His way outward. He is a God that doesn't have borders: Borders for His way of thinking, His plan for your life, His plan for my life.

To be honest, I have used borders in my life. Sometimes it's playing it safe. Sometimes it's to not get hurt (physically, emotionally, and spiritually). Most times, it's to try to convince myself that I'm the one steering the ship.

What I've been learning is the border of shame has been one of the most debilitating, constrictive, and life stealing diseases I have ever been afflicted with. But contrary to what many may believe, it's not incurable.

It will take a skilled surgeon.

It will take some recovery time.

It will take dedicated belief that you can and will get better and be stronger on the other side. It is possible to beat this disease.

It is possible to be healed.

But difficult if not impossible to beat on your own.

If you're frustrated and burnt out from trying to beat things on your own, I've been there. If you feel you can just barely see a sliver of light from somewhere in the back of the cave of shame you're in, I've been there. With every ounce of strength you have, keep your eyes on that light. With laser focus, move toward that light, even if it only feels like a step or two each day. That light is the hope, joy and freedom that only God can offer. Let Jesus break down the borders that hold you in. Let Him put the pieces of your puzzle together the way only He can. There won't be any missing pieces because He already holds them all in His hands.

Our God is a God without borders and when He puts the scattered pieces of a puzzle back together, he works in reverse order. His formula for success = Start with the inside pieces and work His way out.

When we lean on something, it's because we need support. We need its added strength to help us stay strong and balanced. It's hard for me and my male bravado to admit, but sometimes I need to lean on someone other than myself for strength. In these times of complete vulnerability and surrender, when I can say I don't have the answers – that I don't know where the pieces of the puzzle fit, Jesus is there. He wants to be the one we lean on. Even when we don't know what we need, He does.

He sees the puzzle for so much more than scattered and often missing pieces. He sees us as the beautiful masterpiece fashioned by his hand. His lungs breathed us into existence. He sees the big picture.

Trusting God may take time. Talk to Him today and ask Him to show you where you need to lean on Him more. Don't worry or stress if you can't seem to find where all the puzzle pieces fit today. If you let Him, the one who designed the puzzle will show you how the pieces fit to form a masterpiece more beautiful than you could ever imagine. Above all, know Jesus loves you. He is for you and wants the best for your life.

*What pieces don't fit the way you want them to?*

*How can you trust God more with these areas?*

## 22

# THE ATTITUDE AFFECT

———————

I remember watching Winnie the Pooh when I was little and seeing Eeyore chased by his own personal storm cloud. No matter where he goes, it follows him like a shadow. 24/7/365. Soaked to the bone!! The sad thing is, I have noticed myself being this guy from time to time. My brothers would even call me Oscar the Grouch when I was younger.

When I'm trapped beneath my own personal thunderhead, no matter where I run, it follows. And if I run next to anyone else, chances are they will get caught in an unwanted deluge as well (or at least end up with some wet shoes from the puddles).

———

I've used this illustration many times over the years to highlight some important points to others I have worked with in the wellness arena. The beauty (and sometimes the gut punch) is that every time I teach these principles to someone else; I am reminded I need to continue to grow in these areas too.

It's easy to get used to the storm. We as humans, seem to have a negativity bias. The longer the storm is going, the less we notice it. It becomes the norm. This can be a powerful and detrimental thing. You can either stand and get soaked or you can get out your umbrella (i.e., change your attitude). We all have that choice.

Dr. Martin Seligman Ph.D. says, "The focus on negative events sets us up for anxiety and depression."

If this statement is true, then why is it we have such a hard time buying into the fact that the opposite is just as true? If we focus on gratitude and having a positive attitude, even in the midst of the storms of life, we can find peace. This peace is the power of the Holy Spirit living and working in us.

Believe it or not, you're not the only one affected by the rain. Being a daddy to two amazing little kids is one of the most important roles in my life. I love to teach them, spend time with them and help them learn and grow. Being a dad can be frustrating and exhausting at times too.

I can see a change in the attitudes of my kids almost immediately when I'm not paying enough attention to my own.

I can tell a difference in theirs when I'm missing the mark in how I treat their mommy too. If I'm teaching them how important their attitude is (even at a young age), I need to make sure I'm modeling this principle in my life. Not once in a while, but consistently. We need fewer experts and more examples.

What we say is critically important, but our attitude is equally important. John C. Maxwell said it like this *"People may hear your words, but they feel your attitude"*.

Even though I sometimes don't do it well, I try to stay aware of the impact of my attitude on those around me.

A negative attitude narrows your field of vision. Much like driving our car, if we don't adjust our mirrors (how we perceive and engage the surrounding environment), we are afflicted with blind spots. Accidents will result. A negative attitude causes us to lose sight of all the wonder and beauty happening around us every day. If you need to re-read Chapter 10 – Adjust Your Focus, this would be an ideal time to do so.

This is not meant to sound like fluff. It's reality.

We can't allow ourselves to get so consumed by the negative that we lose sight that this life is a gift. We are fearfully and wonderfully made – on purpose and for a purpose.

So today, take some time to adjust your mirrors and expand your field of vision. No matter what you may believe, everything that happens to you is in your best interest. Every opportunity we face, good or bad, is an opportunity for growth. We can either let our circumstances control us or we can use each opportunity to learn and develop a stronger sense of gratitude and patience. Just like the muscles in our body, gratitude and patience develop best when encountered by resistance and struggle.

Deliberate and consistent practice will strengthen you. Our attitude starts with our thoughts. If we are focused on how people have hurt or wronged us, before too long, our hearts grow cold and dry. It's impossible to yield a good crop if the soil isn't rich. It's also impossible to yield a good crop if you aren't planting the right seeds.

Our attitude is just one part of the process of becoming the person we were created to be. If we deliberately focus on this, I believe we will be amazed at what happens. Our attitude can change the environment we live in, the environment we work in and it can change the world.

I am still a work in progress in this category. We all are. But I believe the process of change and growth in my sometimes sub-par attitude is more than worth the effort. I pray that all of us can begin to see how important our attitudes are on our well-being and that of those around us.

# 23

# I LEARN FROM YOU DADDY

———————

Do the right things.

Say this. Don't say that.

Pray at meals and before bed.

Don't ever mess up.

And if you do mess up, pray like crazy, that God will forgive you.

Growing up, this is what I thought it meant to follow Christ. I thought God had a big checklist. One side of pros. One side of cons.

I had religion.

I needed Jesus.

If God's love for us depended on what we did or didn't

do, we would always be on the outside looking in. It depends on our acceptance of the free gift of His salvation and grace. It depends 100% on what Christ has already done for us.

Everything else (our actions, reactions, thoughts, words, behavior) is a byproduct of our dependence on Him and an unquenchable desire to follow Him. We should strive each day, in public (easier to do) and in private (harder to do), to reflect Jesus to everyone we meet. We never know who is watching and learning from us. We never know who we are influencing.

Recently, I was cleaning things in the kitchen at home while Michelle was out running errands. Sometimes as parents we have to divide and conquer! Our daughter was napping and our son was playing in the living room. Out of the blue, he stands up, looks over the ledge between the two rooms and uttered five simple words that made my heart leap with joy and simultaneously sent a shock wave through my soul.

"I learn from you daddy", he said.

It's crazy how something so simple and innocent can have such a profound impact on how we view our world. It made me realize that I need to be aware as a dad that I am not just a dad.

My job is not just to teach and discipline our children, but to be an example of the kind person I hope they become. This is one of the greatest ways I can show them how much I love them. They will do the things that they see me doing. What a huge responsibility. Even Jesus said that he didn't do anything on his own, but only what He saw the Father doing (John 5:19).

My son has done this on more than one occasion. During the process of writing and editing this book, he reminded me again that he is a keen observer of my actions and behaviors. I turned around to find him perched, my glasses sliding down his nose, at dining room table in front of my computer.

"Dad, I just need to work on my book a little", he stated.

I laughed out loud. "What are you doing buddy", I asked.

"Being daddy", he responded matter-of-factly.

This was a great reminder that if you don't think people are listening, they are. Maybe not to your words, but to the way you live your life. It's these small reminders that show me God wants me to take note. These are the things He wants me to remember – the areas He wants me to continue to grow in.

I have heard people so many times justify why they might say or do certain things (I've done this too). To be honest, if I have to research just to prove why I say or do things just to push the envelope, I'm trying to captain my own ship. I've found out that the seas of life are much more treacherous when I'm the one behind the wheel. When we look at The Bible it gives a crystal-clear road map for how we should live. Simple, yes. Easy, no (at least under our power alone).

If who I am and who I am becoming doesn't line up with the Word of God, then I'm not moving in the right direction. What's even more frightening is that I could cause others to move in the wrong direction too. We need to be constantly aware and intentional in how we are fueling our hearts, as well as how that fuel is fanning the flame of our actions and reactions. The fuel we put into our heart and minds affects the production that comes out. It will show up in our lives. Our cars might run on sub-par fuel for a while, but it won't be long until they need some serious repair. Our true character is often revealed when the flames of life get hottest.

What I've realized is that we can and should have this same approach in our relationship with the Father. If we are watching, studying and imitating Him, before long we will act more like Him. If His heart is transplanted in us, we can't help but take on His characteristics:

Love

Joy

Peace

Patience

Kindness

Gentleness

Goodness

Self-Control

Forgiveness

I believe Jesus was 100% man and 100% God. He had a sense of humor and joked with his friends. He endured every temptation we have ever faced or will face without succumbing to sin. I believe too, He embodied things like frustration from time to time. When Jesus was talking with and comforting His disciples after His Resurrection, Philip, one of his disciples, asked Jesus to show them the Father.

———

*Have I been with you all this time, Philip, and yet you still don't know who I am? Anyone who has seen me has seen the Father! So why are you asking me to show him to you? Don't you believe that I am in the Father and the Father is in me? The words I speak are not my own, but my Father who lives in me does his work through me. Just believe that I am in the Father and the Father is in me. Or at least believe because of the work you have seen me do. (John 14:9-11)*

———

I wish I could have heard the inflection in Jesus' voice when He answered. Phillip was one of Jesus' closest friends. He spent almost every waking hour together for over 3 years and still they needed proof. Now He's standing here, back from the dead. If I were Jesus, I would have been like "Phillip, dude, are you kidding me right now?"

When I am talking with God and just spending time with Him, I want to able to look at Him and say, "I learn from you daddy".

They say imitation is the highest form of flattery. I don't

think God needs our flattery but I believe when His children take on His heart and His love he is overjoyed.

# 24

# FEAR VS. LOVE

---

*Everything we do is motivated by either fear or by love.*

Those 11 words spoken by my dad in a sermon shot straight into my brain with deadly accuracy. It penetrated deeper as he repeated the statement two more times. In the back of my head, I could hear the voice of a teacher I had years ago telling me, if he repeated something more than once in class, it was worth writing down. So that is what I did.

*Everything we do is motivated by either fear or by love.*

God many times works the same way in our lives. He may not expect us to scribble down these lessons in our college ruled notebook, but he definitely wants us to listen, remember, and most importantly, apply. For me, I know He sometimes has to repeat Himself more than once to get me to take note.

Reading this countless times over the next couple of months I realized, that shot didn't just hit my brain, it hit my heart.

*Everything we do is motivated by either fear or by love.*

1 John 4:17-18 in the Message version of the Bible puts it like this:

---

*God is love. When we take up permanent residence in a life of love, we live in God and God lives in us. This way, love has the run of the house, becomes at home and mature in us, so we're free of worry on Judgment Day—our standing in the world is identical with Christ's. There is no room in love for fear. Well-formed love banishes fear. Since fear is crippling, a fearful life—fear of death, fear of judgment—is one not yet fully formed in love. (John 4:17-18 MSG)*

---

Fear forces.

Love serves.

Fear stops us dead in our tracks.

Love is the catalyst that propels us forward.

Fear is a powerful emotion and it can play an important role in our lives. But we have to put it into perspective.

Fear can serve as a healthy boundary to protect us from

harm. Every time our little girl is close to the stove, she says "hot". She knows if she touches the burner, it will hurt.

Fear can operate as a barometer of respect. I have a healthy fear of God. His ways and thoughts are higher than mine (Isaiah 55:8–9). The fear of the Lord is the foundation of wisdom (Proverbs 9:10). He is the creator and I am His creation. Enough said.

Fear however, is also the single greatest factor that cripples us into believing we have limited potential in this beautiful gift of life we've been given.

Fear is selfish.

Fear is not your friend.

Fear is from the enemy.

Fear is a prison.

Love is the key.

*Everything we do is motivated by either fear or by love.*

We live in a world infatuated with the novelty of love. What we don't realize though, is the novelty of love isn't as powerful as the intimacy of love. We are called to intimacy.

Living true to the path of intimacy in our relationships can be difficult. It requires work, upkeep, patience, and perseverance. It requires sacrifice.

If any of our relationships (God, marriage, friendships, etc.) are motivated by fear, they will always be dysfunctional. A leader worth following doesn't lead with fear, but with love. Jesus always led with love. We must do the same. Love will open doors that ambition never could.

When our relationships are motivated by love they will have the ability and the freedom to thrive.

No matter what anyone might tell you, we all, deep down at the soul level, want to be loved. As humans, we crave it. It has become increasingly hard, in a sin sick world where love has been twisted and perverted, to let another person know us intimately enough to love us unconditionally. It has even become more difficult to love ourselves.

What are we so afraid of?

There is one who can break this cycle. One who came with a mission rooted in love. There is one who is wrapped in the DNA of love.

Love is our provider.

Love is our protector.

Love is the single most powerful agent of change this world will ever know.

Love is our only hope.

Jesus is love.

Jesus isn't our religion. Jesus is our Savior. Jesus is our Lord. Because we are created in His image, Jesus has called us to be love. He has passed the torch to us. And he is calling us to evolve in how we understand and show love.

I love this quote by Joshua Medcalf in his book Chop Wood Carry Water[1]:

---

1. Chop Wood Carry Water: How to Fall in Love with The Process of Becoming Great

*"Every day I'm learning how to fuel my heart & starve my fears. Love attracts energy. Fear consumes it."*

---

It is imperative that every day we must focus on what fuels our heart. What we listen to, what we read, what we watch, the conversations we engage in, how we spend our time—all of these things either fill our tanks up or run them dry.

We all need to ask ourselves:

What kind of fuel am I using?

What am I motivated by?

Am I operating paralyzed by fear or propelled by love?

Am I building on a strong foundation of love or a faulty foundation of fear?

## 25

# SAYING GOODBYE TO PERFECTIONISM

———————

Most of us never forget our first love. I know I won't. I will never forget how she smelled or how I felt when I was around her. It was as if no one else in the world mattered. I wanted to spend the rest of my life with her. Her name was Baseball. We shared so many fond memories. And if I could go back, I would in a heartbeat.

Unfortunately, I gave up on her before our relationship could blossom into something more long term or exclusive. My excuses were simple. I said I didn't like the coach I would soon have. And anyway, it took up too much time and I just wanted to enjoy being a kid. I still regret this decision every time I step onto a baseball field.

It is hard for me to admit, but many times, I only gave enough effort to perform well and escape the trap of being seen as a failure (on the field and off). Admitting my diagnosis to the masses (or even just my family – even scarier) is the first step to moving toward wholeness and the purpose for my life that God intended.

I've lived most of my life with a fear of people finding out I'm a fraud – that I might not be who I say I am.

I've wrestled with the reality of failure.

It's crippling. It's as if someone has tied a 10 ton stone around your foot and thrown you into the water to swim with the fishes.

As the oldest of 4 brothers, I felt it was my inborn nature to do everything right. I was supposed to set the standard. I thought I had to be the best on the court, the track, the diamond or in the classroom. What I didn't realize, was I was the only one who believed this.

In reality, I had let others' perceived expectations of me become my driver – my "motivation". The effort needed to pursue excellence and grow had taken a very abrupt backseat. Actually, I had told it to sit in the back and keep its mouth shut. It was easier to give up "on my terms" than to show weakness. To truly be the person I was created to be I would have to undergo a massive surgery to treat this disease of perfection in my life before it became the posture of my heart.

I didn't want to admit my struggles – that I had weaknesses. I didn't know at the time that when our weaknesses are exposed, we have an opportunity to become stronger. We know where we need to focus; especially if we have the right guidance.

Like a stow away, this mindset followed me into adulthood and into my marriage. Carrying the weight of perfectionism is hard. What I didn't realize was that the more I tried to carry it, the more my wife was getting crushed under the weight too. I had to unload it. Jesus was the spotter I needed to help me lift the weight off before it crushed me.

Perfection is a myth.

Perfection is a disease.

Perfection is unattainable.

Perfection is a dying commodity, but the demand for excellence is on the rise. Excellence is something worth striving for. Excellence is within our reach and control.

Perfectionism is our feeble attempt to raise the bar to such unattainable heights and by our own effort, trying to do what only God can do! Our unwillingness to admit we are broken combined with the perceived expectations of others, leads to a vicious cycle that looks like this:

*Broken and seeking approval →perceived expectations of others → trying through our effort/seeking validation →not happy with responses →work harder to make others happy →become less happy with ourselves.*

Wash. Rinse. Repeat.

This has become the cycle for many of us today. It's no wonder we aren't happy with the lives we are living. I know my shoulders aren't strong enough to carry the weight of perfectionism. Believe me, I found this out first hand.

The Apostle Paul told us:

---

*Each time He said, "My grace is all you need. My power works best in weakness." So now I am glad to boast about my weaknesses, so that the power of Christ can work through me. (2 Corinthians 12:9)*

---

Jesus didn't call us to be perfect. He called us to follow Him and let Him be perfect for us.

So how do we begin to begin to say goodbye to perfectionism in our lives?

1. <u>Realize we are in control of our effort</u>: We are the only ones who can make the choices we make. No one else can make us work any harder than we choose to work. This holds true in our practices, our studies, our careers, our marriages, etc. Once this truth takes root in our heart, it will catch fire. The fire that spreads will burn brighter and hotter than you can imagine when you are the one striking the match.

2. <u>Don't blame others. Take responsibility</u>: We try to point to external factors as the reason we don't

improve or perform well. We all want exposure but we oftentimes wear the mask of fear because we are afraid of being exposed. We fear the judgment of not being perfect. This will have massive impact in all areas of our lives. Our marriages, our careers, our parenting, etc. Focus on giving your best effort. Control your attitude. Pursue excellence...one day at a time.

3. <u>Realize that sometimes we all fall off of the horse</u>: It's OK to fail. It's not the end. This is the time to learn and grow. Enough said.

4. <u>Believe you are worth the excellence you're chasing</u>: There will be times in your life where you may be the only one who believes in you. That's OK. Stay faithful and consistent. You're worth comes from who you are, not because you're perfect at something. Don't chase notoriety. Chase excellence in love and in the pursuit of your purpose.

Believe in the process. Say goodbye to perfectionism before it takes up permanent residence in your life. We all have excellence inside of us. It's up to each of us to decide whether or not we chase it.

# 26

# SHAKEN, NOT STIRRED

---

I love James Bond Movies. Old ones, new ones, it doesn't matter. I love them all. Bond, James Bond is the ultimate cool in my book. He never cracks under pressure no matter the circumstance. He always has a plan and a way out. Not to mention, some insanely cool toys!

When I was younger, if TNT, USA, FX or any other network played a Bond marathon, I was glued to the TV. It didn't even matter who was playing Bond, although I will argue that Sean Connery is by far the best. Daniel Craig is giving him a run for his money though.

I think the allure of Bond for me though, is pure escapism.

---

He always has an answer.

*I sometimes don't.... OK, most of the time I don't.*

He has a witty comeback.

*Some things sound much better in my head.*

James always gets the girl.

*I might be a little biased, but my bride is hotter than any Bond girl.*

I know however, that James' life is nothing more than a script. A fabrication, made up by a writer who is most likely living vicariously through his scripts as much as me, and many others do watching Bond on film.

The more that I search after God's heart, I find that as nice as it would be to have a life that is smooth sailing, no bumps in the road, easy as Sunday morning, or any other cliché you want to insert here — wait for it...LIFE ISN'T ALWAYS THIS WAY!!

It's more often like a road that always seems to be under construction. If you live or have driven anywhere around the areas of St. Louis that I have, you know what I mean (Interstate 64 anyone)! It isn't always mixed gently with the turn of a spoon (like the milk in my coffee, no sweetener). It isn't always STIRRED.

So many times, life feels like all its ingredients have been thrown into a martini shaker, mixed up without reason and then strained into the glass to see what results (please hold the olive). And sometimes, ingredients we would not have included in our recipe are added. Life can feel SHAKEN (as is Bond's method of choice).

Jesus never said life would be easy. In fact, He said the exact opposite. The apostle Paul told us we would have to "deny ourselves daily" (Luke 9:23) to follow Christ. Jesus himself told us that "you will be hated all over the world because you are my followers".

That doesn't sound like much fun but it sure beats an eternal hangover!!

Lately, this concept of being SHAKEN has been what has been driving me – the challenge of the unknown. The thirst to know God and myself on a deeper, more intimate level has moved into the driver's seat. This is scary and freeing at the same time. I am learning that the more I am SHAKEN, the more God is revealing himself to me – teaching me, preparing me.

Great Sacrifice = Great Reward

So, if you're up for the challenge, let's go out and have a life together. Shaken not stirred.

The first round is on me!! No designated driver required.

27

# SCRIBBLE SCRABBLE

One of the things I love most about being a parent is that I get to engage in all the activities I did when I was a kid (if I'm honest though at just slightly south of 40, I'm still just a big kid). What's cool is, no one looks at me funny when I'm sitting with my two pint-sized sidekicks playing with play dough, watching cartoons, or one of the favorites at our house – coloring.

There is something cathartic about pressing those crayons, markers or colored pencils to the paper and seeing the picture come to life before your eyes. Even if it is only Elsa, Anna or Olaf from Disney's Frozen.

One day, when our son was coloring he got outside of

the lines – outside of the neatly drawn, pre-defined pictures on the page. There were actually more colors outside of the lines than inside them. When he did this, he looked at my wife and me and declared, "that's scribble scrabble".

He said it like he had messed up. Like it wasn't OK to color outside of the lines. As my wife and I have thought and talked about that statement, my perspective has changed greatly. My thinking began to drift outside of the pre-defined mindset I had and didn't even realize.

First of all, at the time, Cohen was only three years old. Coloring outside of the lines is natural – it's OK. It will not make or break the outcome of his future if he colors the sun blue or the grass purple. I've grown to enjoy watching him and our daughter scribble on the pages. And sometimes my wife and I encouraging them to. It may seem small and insignificant, but if we force our kids to stay inside the lines now, we could stifle their imaginations – their creativity. If we aren't careful, this can have a long lasting and not necessarily positive influence on their lives as they get older . We want them to use the imaginations they were given to dream. The possibilities are endless!

Why do we try to get kids to color inside of the lines, anyway?

Are we scared to let them create?

Are we scared they will face ridicule?

Are we scared they will fall behind?

Do we think that we are showing them how to be successful?

Are we teaching them to stay inside the lines because that's what we were taught?

Do we think that if they color outside of the lines and others see it, that it will be a reflection on us?

Jesus colored outside of the lines. He came and disrupted everything that the world believed. He painted with an abstract but simple approach. He came to love and to serve.

People who have colored outside of the lines have not only contributed improvements and innovations in our world, but have also shaped the course of our history.

Hundreds of thousands of songs have been written on the guitar alone using just 4 chords. That's doesn't even take into consideration the countless number that have been written from the minor and dissonant chords – the open and alternate tunings.

Each of us are just alternate tunings. Each one of us is designed to create and play a unique song – to bring a unique and beautiful sound into this world. Use your voice, your gifts, your abilities, your creativity, your vision, your story. We are meant to leave a mark on this world. Not only one that says we were here, but to serve as an imprint of the Creator. We are called to create – to leave the world a better place for those who come after us. If we always color inside of the lines, this is close to impossible.

Let's face it, with a limited color palette, this life world be pretty boring.

How many more ideas, inventions and innovations can be created by the millions of brain cells, unique in each of us? Don't color inside the lines. It's OK to scribble scrabble, – to mix different colors, to use different materials. Who makes the rules that tell us we can't, anyway? We weren't designed to conform. We were designed to create. Let your imagination run wild on the playground of creativity. Let your thoughts pluck the strings of the synapses of your brain, creating a symphony that sounds unique to the call God has placed on your life. A guitar string can only sing when put under tension. So why do we run from it? I encourage all of us to press in to the tension today and see what kind of beautiful song can result.

Don't be sacred to scribble scrabble – to color outside of the lines. When God created all of existence from a blank canvas, there weren't any lines to stay inside. He spoke everything into being. He just created. We are created in the image of God. That space just outside of the lines is waiting to be discovered.

# 28

# THE WAITING

---

I really suck at the waiting – waiting in traffic, waiting for my food when we are out to dinner or waiting for the kids to go to bed (especially on nights when all I want to do is sit and spend some uninterrupted adult time with my wife). Needless to say, I'm a work in progress. And I'm OK with that.

This following phrase has taught me why the waiting is so important.

---

*One of the greatest determinants of our success is our <u>ability</u> and <u>willingness</u> to delay gratification.*

---

We all have the ability to delay gratification. Being willing to do it, well, that's a little more challenging.

Today we want everything a click away. We want an instant download. Because let's face it. That's how the world works, right? Try again.

One of my favorite examples of having the ability *and* willingness to delay gratification is King David. The prophet Samuel was sent to anoint the next King of Israel as a successor to King Saul (1 Samuel 16:1-13). After meeting all of Jesse's sons he still hadn't met the one who God said would be the one (and no, it wasn't Neo from the Matrix).

Jesse's youngest son David was out in the field tending the sheep. He was just a shepherd. What qualifications did this kid have to be the next King of a great nation? Samuel asked to see him anyway.

God told Samuel that this kid, this teenager, this shepherd was the anointed one. He even went so far as to say he had a heart just like God's. Talk about a compliment and some big shoes to fill!

So, at 15 years old, surrounded by the smell of sheep in a field, young David was anointed as the next King of Israel. This transition didn't happen immediately though. He wouldn't take the throne for another 15 years!

15 *more years* of watching sheep graze in the pasture.

15 *more years* of sleeping out in the fields under the stars, instead of in the palace.

15 *more years* of sitting in the fields, playing music to the

sheep before he would pen some of the most beautiful songs ever crafted (Psalms).

*15 more years* of being picked on by his 7 older brothers.

*15 more years* of respecting the authority he was under until he could be in a place of authority over Israel.

*15 more years* of honing not just his craft but *honing his heart.*

Until then, he was faithful with the things entrusted to him. He remained steady and focused on what he had to do each day. He knew the process was where he would grow and be refined into the man who would someday take the throne. He had to train and be faithful with the small things before he could be blessed to lead an empire.

*It was all about David's heart posture* – not his potential, talent, or ability. It wasn't about his failures either (and he would have some big ones). God saw the posture of David's heart and that was his greatest strength.

Would I have the ability and willingness to wait 15 years for what I knew would be a promotion like no other? Would I wait 15 years to fulfill the purpose that God had placed in my heart and on my life? I have a hard time waiting 15 minutes for my meal if I'm out to dinner. David waited for 15 years knowing he would someday be king! This definitely puts my rumbling stomach into perspective.

David wrote one of the most prolific prayers of all time in Psalm 23:1-6:

*The Lord is my shepherd;*
*I have all that I need.*
*He lets me rest in green meadows;*
*he leads me beside peaceful streams.*
*He renews my strength.*
*He guides me along right paths,*
*bringing honor to his name.*
*Even when I walk*
*through the darkest valley,*
*I will not be afraid,*
*for you are close beside me.*
*Your rod and your staff*
*protect and comfort me.*
*You prepare a feast for me*
*in the presence of my enemies.*
*You honor me by anointing my head with oil.*
*My cup overflows with blessings.*
*Surely your goodness and unfailing love will pursue me*
*all the days of my life,*
*and I will live in the house of the Lord*
*forever. (Psalms 23:1-6)*

What is it about his words that still have the power today they had when he first penned them? Even then, we see he knew there was power and benefit in the waiting.

David wasn't worried about the future. He didn't worry if he would have shelter, food, or clothes. He didn't have to rush out on black Friday to get the door buster deals and beat the flocks of people (pun intended) trying to beat him there. He knew as long as his heart posture was focused on the Lord, all the other things didn't really matter. By having the one thing he truly needed, all the other things of the world became secondary. He knew what his "first things" were.

There was a time in my life when I thought that moving to a new city would help me escape the pain that I was going through. Instead of opening the door for my escape, God told me to stay. It wasn't time yet. He wanted me to learn that the waiting was important. There were some weeds He wanted to start to burn away and some hurts he wanted to heal. This couldn't happen if, like a fugitive, I was trying to outrun my situation. Sometimes we have to stay in the waiting place until it's time for us to propel forward into new territory.

What are the areas of your life where you have the ability to delay gratification but the willingness is lacking?

Be bold!

Write them down.

Pray about them.

Will you take the time to slow down and listen to His voice?

We don't always know what's going on behind the scenes. I am notorious for wanting to analyze all the details. I want to see the reason for the work to be done. The waiting is when all the elements are being prepared and put into place. If we pull the trigger to soon, before everything is loaded, things may be incomplete. We may miss the target. Product before process can be a dangerous formula (remember the importance of the foundation).

This was a hard lesson for me to learn. This also applies to our perception of the heart posture of others. We need to be careful not to judge others based on our perception, or how we want them to act (be cut from a religious cookie cutter). We don't know how the Lord may be working on their hearts. We don't know where they are on their journey. They may be in a waiting period themselves. Maybe you are in a waiting period right now.

We need to view our challenges during the waiting as opportunities to grow. We should strive to continually improve, no matter what things look like now, or even what they may look like in the future. Let your effort flow from your heart. Stay true to the purpose God has placed there and watch what happens! You can't see fruit if you don't plant, water, and tend to the seeds.

We need to enjoy the waiting period. The waiting is when we train and hone our gifts and abilities.

This is where we learn what we are made of.

It is where we are refined.

This is where true success is planted, takes root, and matures.

Please wear your seat belt because there will be bumps in the road. But above all, enjoy the ride.

Above all, don't mistake God's silence for absence.

Sometimes He may sit back to watch and see if we are putting to work the lessons He is teaching. But He is always there. He will never leave us. God has and still does amazing things in and through people who trust Him, even in the waiting. It so easy to ask God why he isn't showing and telling us what to do in the waiting. I heard Pastor Joe Smith from Mosaic Church LA say this:

*"Too many times we ask God why He isn't telling us what we should do. But God is asking us why we haven't been listening to Him when He was."*

If you feel you're in a holding pattern wondering what's next, pray, trust, and focus during the waiting. Hone and tune your heart into the beat of God's, and believe He will use you in amazing ways for His glory. Don't be in such a hurry to move into the palace that you forget about the process it takes to get there.

## 29

# SLEEPING ON THE FLOOR

As I said earlier, parenting is one thing in life that no matter how ready you think you are, you can never be fully prepared for. I remember sitting at a Meineke in Sacramento, CA waiting to get an oil change for my car when this became increasingly clear.

I was sitting in the waiting room drinking my second pot of coffee for the day (slightly higher than my average, but I was a new dad), when I overheard the news on the TV. Our son was only about 9 or 10 months old at the time and needless to say, sleep was definitely higher on my wife's and my priority list than it was on his. The fact I even heard the TV or could focus on it was a miracle.

"In the first year of an infant's life, new parents lose on average 40 days of sleep," the anchor said.

*24 hours x 40 days = 960 hours.*

I just laughed and shrugged my shoulders. "That's seems about right" I said, nodding in agreement.

Cohen eventually began sleeping through the night (thank you nighttime diapers). But as all of you parents will find out, these periods will come in waves. Just when you feel you're hitting you're stride, things will take a very abrupt left turn.

I absolutely love being a dad. It is one of the things that brings me the most joy in this beautiful life I've been given. That being said, it does has its challenging moments. Even through those times I wouldn't trade it for anything in the world.

When Cohen was almost 2 years old (he's 4 at the printing of this book), he was going through one of those challenging times and having an incredibly hard time going to sleep at night. This resulted in Michelle and I having an incredibly hard time going to sleep at night as well. Every night was a mental and physical challenge. I'm positive that neither of us could have gotten through without the strength of God.

During one of these bouts with our son, I was just about at the peak of physical and mental exhaustion. He was fighting sleep with the ferocity of Muhammad Ali's punches. I wanted to turn my dad card back in and was wondering if I was cut out for fatherhood.

I remember losing my cool and telling him I just wanted him to go to sleep, more intensely than I should have. Just because I wanted to go to sleep myself. Thinking back on this moment in time still makes me shudder.

As soon as the words came out of my mouth, the Holy Spirit hit me with a right cross that knocked me to the canvas.

"Joe, how many times have you been crying at night for me to pick you up and hold your hand? Have I ever told you just go to sleep because I was tired?"

I hit the floor by my son's bed, tears flowing down my cheeks. I think I got up before the 10 count, but my head was definitely spinning. As I pulled myself up, my son had his hand stuck through the rails of his crib saying "Daddy, hold my hand".

I crumpled.

"Of course buddy, Daddy will hold your hand," I told him.

What I've realized is that when either our son or daughter are going through the stormy sea of sleepless nights (or other concerns as they get older), they need comfort. They need to know they are safe. They need to know mommy and daddy are there for them. They need to know mommy and daddy are in the boat with them. Sometimes it means sleeping on the floor next to the bed. Sometimes, for our daughter, it's been just placing my hand on her back and singing to her.

I want them to know they are safe and secure.

They need safety and security.

We need safety and security.

I need safety and security.

Not just for peace of mind, but for peace in our souls.

Our Heavenly father is always here to be that and so much more for us. Even when we are trying to navigate our sleepless nights and stormy seas, He will never forcefully tell us to just go to sleep. He will be there to hold our hands and wrap His arms around us. He will provide comfort and rest in Him—even in the storms.

# 30

# YOU DON'T DESERVE GRACE...AND NEITHER DO I

Man, sometimes being a parent is hard work. I feel like this has been a theme of several of these chapters. I've been thinking a lot about this lately, because God has been using our children to teach me more about how His love really works and about the condition of my own heart.

Not too long ago my wife and I were talking about disciplining our kids. She pointed out that I have a much different approach with our son than I do with our daughter. At times I have less patience when disciplining our son than with our daughter. It's not very conducive to helping him learn and grow. Honestly it's sometimes more about just *getting* him to obey vs. *teaching* why obedience is beneficial.

At first, I got defensive. After I listened to what she was saying and her heart behind it, my perspective shifted.

I had great parents growing up. I am forever grateful for that. However, my dad and I butted heads on many different occasions, probably because we are a lot alike. Despite the occasional struggles, I knew my dad loved me and only wanted the best for me and to teach me. I know he still feels this way today. Because of this, we have a great relationship (I love you Pop).

Some of the patterns of the struggles I had with my dad when I was younger, I was beginning to see with my son. The balancing act of being his authority figure, teacher, disciplinarian and friend is kind of like walking a tightrope in a circus. You might start out with total confidence, but just a little movement in the rope changes your focus, approach and confidence. When you add in a second child, with a different personality + work + being a husband + providing for a family + helping take care of our home can feel like trying to juggle chainsaws while walking the tightrope. There can be a pretty small margin of error.

What God has been teaching me is that even though I need to discipline and teach our kids (the teaching is harder sometimes), my mission isn't just to make them listen because I say so.

I want them to know they have a choice. I want them to know I love them regardless – even if I may not agree sometimes with their choices. Just like the father in the story of the prodigal son, they will always be welcomed with open arms. This is the same way that Jesus loves each of us when we come home – with open arms and full of love and forgiveness even if He doesn't like some of the choices we've made along the way. I never want to use the phrase "because I'm dad, and I said so".

I need to show them I love them despite what they do. My love isn't based on their actions – if they obey or not. It's based on the fact that I love them because they are my children. Their identity as my children won't ever change, no matter what they do. Neither will my love for them.

That's how God feels about each of us. He doesn't love us because He has to. He loves us because He loves us. Our identity isn't about what we do. It's about who God is and how He views us.

We don't really deserve the grace we've been given, but God gives it anyway. It's up to us to decide if we want to take Him up on His offer. He wants our hearts to look just like His. Hopefully by the end of this book we are all inching closer to that destination.

## 31

# WRAPPING UP

—————

If you've made it this far, I want to say thank you. Thank you for taking the time to read. Thank you for taking the time to look into your own heart the way God has been challenging me to look into mine. I pray that you allow Him to show you the areas of old growth that need to be burned away in order for you to live the life you were created for. I pray that you let God issue a controlled burn on those areas. I pray that you become a spark and burn even brighter in this world.

The journey we are all on in this life – the circumstances that surround us, where we were born, the opportunities afforded to us – are all different. The path that we walk and the challenges and victories we face are all different too. I can't say your journey will be like or turn out like mine. But I know God loves you, even if you can't see it right now. And that's OK. He will never force himself on you.

He has revealed some areas in my life through writing this book. And sometimes the fire He has started hurt at first. But it was necessary. I will probably feel that fire again because it is a never-ending process.

If you are just discovering Jesus for the first time, I'm excited for you. I wish I could promise you it will be an easy and perfect road but I can't. There will be lonely times. I've felt them. There will be times of doubt. I've been there too. But I can tell you he will never leave you or forsake you. He will always be there to wrap His loving arms around you, no matter what.

For those of you who aren't for sure about Jesus; thank you for reading. I hope you found encouragement in these pages – in the lessons I'm still in the process of learning myself. I hope that these words have planted a seed inside of you and you begin to see yourself in a brighter light. You matter to me and are loved – unconditionally.

Wherever you are at, I would like to invite you to pray this prayer with me.

*Jesus, thank you for your unconditional love. Thank you for creating me. Thank you for giving your life for me. Thank you for your forgiveness. Show me the areas of my heart that I need you to burn away so that I can live the life you created me for.*

*Amen.*

# Because of YOUs

*To Michelle:* You are my inspiration, my heart and my soul. You are truly my GOOD THING. If it weren't for you, I may have never had the courage and boldness to let God begin a controlled burn on my heart. You are the definition of a Heart Arsonist. You seek the truth above all else and settle for nothing less. Thank you for the way you love fiercely, serve selflessly, and always strive to represent the true heart of the Father. I am honored to burn alongside you in this life and I pray that our flames only burn brighter over time. Our journey to where we are today was full of twists and turns, but I wouldn't trade that route for anything. Each speed bump and pothole was worth it to arrive at our destination. Because of YOU I believed this book was possible. Because of YOU I believe anything is possible. The journey is far from over, so buckle up baby!! I love yo...Always and Forever.

*To Cohen (our priest and protector) and Annalee (our princess with a heart of gold):* You have both showed me what it means to have the heart of the Father. You have changed me in ways you will probably never know, but I hope the legacy I leave will echo for a lifetime through both of you. Always remember who you are and more importantly, *whose* you are. Never lose your sense of compassion, your heart of worship or your love for others. Above all, hang onto your childlike faith with white knuckles. **Because of YOU** I found my childlike faith again. Daddy loves you with all my heart and soul.

*To my parents (Bill and Glenda Raby):* Thank you for modeling for me, my bros and everyone who you encounter, what it means to truly live for Jesus. Your wisdom and courage in the face of adversity and consistency to God's call has affected so many. I am forever grateful for the foundation and legacy you built for us. Thank you for teaching me, guiding me, allowing me to fail and for being there to help me learn through the process. I didn't get to choose you as parents, but even if I had gotten that chance, I wouldn't change a thing. **Because of YOU** I am the man I am today. I love you guys more than you will ever know or could be expressed in words.

*To my brothers (Jeremy, Justin, Jonathan, Steve and Dave):* I am honored to call you family. It brings my heart so much joy to see each of you walking in the purpose that God has for each of you. I will never forget or take for granted the life we've lived together. You are 5 of the brightest sparks I know. Because of YOU I am stronger than I knew I could be.

*To Gramps and Mammie (David and Lynda Rands):* Thank you for your constant source of encouragement, wisdom, and love. Because of YOU I have seen what it means to love without judgment and always seek to find the best in people.

*To Joshua Medcalf:* Thanks for your encouragement and willingness to speak the truth. Because of YOU I remembered to not get so focused on the product that I lost sight of the process

*To everyone who has had a hand and a voice in my life (this list would be longer than the book itself – so if you think this is about you, it probably is):* THANK YOU! Because of YOU I want to become more like Jesus every day and pray that my thoughts, words, action and reactions – everything I am – point people to the one who created us all.

*To anyone who has read or will read these words (future heart arsonists):* I hope you are encouraged, inspired and challenged to let The Lord issue a controlled burn on your life so you can have the relationship with Him that He wants and we all so desperately need. Thank YOU for venturing into my heart and life and examining what the Holy Spirit has been teaching. Because of YOU this world will burn brighter with the hope and heart of Jesus Christ!!

*To Jesus Christ – my Lord, my Savior, and my King:* My life is Because of YOU and I give it all back to you now and every day. Your undeserved grace is a gift so infinitely priceless and I am honored that you would love me. I pray that every day my life and my love looks more and more like you. Thank you for igniting my heart. I pray with all I am that I am a good return on your investment.

# My Soundtrack

These songs are just a few of the many on repeat during the writing of this book. They provided encouragement and fuel to my heart along the way. I would encourage you to purchase these songs (the artists deserve it!) and add them to your playlist. The things that we listen to are a vital part of helping shape not only our thoughts, but our hearts and souls as well.

"Touch the Sky" by Hillsong United off of the album Of Dirt and Grace

"The House of God, Forever" by Jon Foreman off of the album Summer

"I Won't Let You Go" by Switchfoot off of the album Where the Light Shines Through

"Fear" by Blue October off of the album Sway

"I Still Haven't Found What I'm Looking For" by U2 off of the album The Joshua Tree (*do yourself a huge favor and just buy this entire album!*

"Yahweh" by Elevation Worship off of the album Here as in Heaven

"Resurrecting" by Elevation Worship off of the album Here as in Heaven

"Sun and Moon" by Phil Wickham off of the album Response

"More Heart, Less Attack" by NeedToBreathe off of the album Rivers in the Wasteland

"Washed by the Water" by NeedToBreathe off of the album The Outsiders

"Storm" by Lifehouse off of the album Who We Are

"Flight" by Lifehouse off of the album Out of the Wasteland

"Tremble" by Mosaic MSC off of the album Glory and Wonder

"Set a Fire" by Jesus Culture off of the album Live in New York

"The Wick" by Housefires off of the Album Housefires III

"That Great Day" by Jonny Lang off of the album Turn Around

"Praise the Lord" by Crowder off of the album American Prodigal

"Test My Faith" by Gandhi's Gun of the album Subject to Change

# About the Author

Hi there. I'm Joe (or Joe Joe if you talk to my wife). I'm a husband to an amazing woman and a daddy to two amazing kids. I have a bordering on unhealthy addiction to coffee. I still think Bon Jovi is one of the best bands ever, and take every opportunity I can to sing their tunes as loud as I can when I'm in the car by myself (don't judge me). Most importantly, I love Jesus with all that I am.

I grew up primarily in and around the small town of Benton, IL. To me, it's still where my roots run deepest. If you ask me, I will tell you that I have a little bit of gypsy blood in me. After living in Grayville, IL, McLeansboro, IL, Hannibal, MO, Marion, IL, Ewing, IL, Zieglar, IL, Macedonia, IL, Edwardsville, Il, Collinsville, IL, St. Louis, MO, Murray, KY and Lexington, KY all before moving to Northern California, you can see why. I currently live in Sacramento, CA with my wife Michelle and our two children – Cohen (4) and Annalee (2).

Made in the USA
Lexington, KY
13 July 2017